Rationalism and Anti-rationalism in the Origins of Economics

To my parents

Rationalism and Anti-rationalism in the Origins of Economics

The Philosophical Roots of 18th Century Economic Thought

William Oliver Coleman
Department of Economics
University of Tasmania
Australia

Edward Elgar

Published by
Edward Elgar Publishing Limited
Gower House
Croft Road
Aldershot
Hants GU11 3HR
England

Edward Elgar Publishing Company
Old Post Road
Brookfield
Vermont 05036
USA

British Library Cataloguing in Publication Data

Coleman, William Oliver
    Rationalism and Anti-rationalism in the Origins of Economics:
    Philosophical Roots of 18th Century Economic Thought
    I. Title
    330.01

Library of Congress Cataloguing in Publication Data

Coleman, William Oliver, 1959–
    Rationalism and anti-rationalism in the origins of economics: the
    philosophical roots of 18th century economic thought / William
    Oliver Coleman
    192p. 22cm.
        1. Economics—History—18th century. 2. Economics—Philosophy.
    I. Title
    HB83.C65 1995   94–45019
    330.1—dc20   CIP

ISBN 1 85278 995 6

Printed and bound in Great Britain by Ipswich Book Co. Ltd., Ipswich, Suffolk

Contents

Acknowledgements

My thanks are due to the early encouragement of Professor Allen Oakley; and to the constructive criticisms of earlier drafts by Professor Peter Groenewegen, Professor John Creedy and Bob Rutherford; and to the participants in the seminar of the Philosophy Department of the University of Tasmania; and to the financial assistance of the Strategic Research Fund of the Faculty of Commerce and Economics of the University of Tasmania, and of the Internal Grants Committee of the Victoria University of Wellington; and to Peter Jones for his technical assistance, and Debbie Johnston for her editorial advice; and to Tracy Kostiuk and Jillian Enraght-Moony for their typing. I would also like to express my gratitude for the painstaking advice of Hilary Fawcett and Christiane Bostock regarding the French translations.

1. Introduction

This is a study of the philosophical roots of economics. It is a study of the impact on economics in its period of origin of two opposing philosophical outlooks: rationalism and anti-rationalism. These two philosophic alternatives had wrangled with one another for about two thousand years when, late in the 17th century, their differences were made sharper by the intellectual upheaval of that period. At that time the first shoots of scientific economics also appeared. This book is about how in the subsequent century the development of economic thought was affected by the renewed rivalry between the two philosophic outlooks. The thesis is that the economics of the 18th century bears the imprint of the discord between rationalism and anti-rationalism. It is to some degree a compound of the two.

This topic is not only of historical interest. The disputes that quickened in the 18th century retain life today. Neoclassical economics is in part (but not wholly) a rationalist enterprise. The criticisms of neoclassical economics are in part (but not wholly) criticisms of its rationalist properties, including the assumptions of optimization, rational expectations and equilibrium. In the controversy over neoclassical economics rationalists and anti-rationalists remain in conflict. This study digs into the intellectual archaeology of this controversy, and hopes to give it some perspective.

1.1 Rationalism and anti-rationalism: a sketch

But what is meant by rationalism? To Lovejoy 'rationalism' is one of those 'trouble-breeding and usually thought-obscuring terms, which one sometimes wishes to see expunged from the vocabulary of philosophy altogether ...' (Lovejoy, 1964, p.6). This book springs from a different opinion. But the term 'rationalism' does need clarification. It is not a single idea. It is collection of doctrines, some of which are concerned with the general nature of the world, some with the sources of knowledge, some with human nature. We shall deal first with the doctrines concerning the general nature of the world. For want of a better term, we shall call these doctrines 'metaphysical'.

'Metaphysics'

To rationalists the world is a structure, not an anarchy. It is a system, not a chaos. This structure is commonly supposed by rationalists to be a *structure of hierarchy*. Certain phenomena are supposed to be the bottom of everything. These foundational realities support other realities, which in turn support others. Descartes provided a classic expression of this view: 'The whole of philosophy is like a tree. The roots are metaphysics, the trunk is physics, and the branches emerging from the trunk, are all the other sciences, ... namely medicine, mechanics and morals' (Descartes, 1985, volume 1, p.186). In the 18th century, however, an alternative rationalist conception of the structure of reality emerged: a *structure of mutual interdependence*. In this conception there is no independent foundational reality on which other realities rest; instead all the various realities support and balance one another. In the 18th century this structure of mutual interdependence was detected in the solar system, international diplomacy, political constitutions, the human mind and the economy.

Since the world is a structure, rationalists must maintain that any disorderly appearance of the world is deceptive. A large part of observed variability is only apparent: the reality is uniform. The ancient Platonic expression of this claim was that observed variability is just a flickering shadow of immutable realities existing outside the ordinary world. Enlightenment rationalism brought these uniform realities out of that strange Platonic heaven and put them into the ordinary everyday world. To the 18th century, for example, men, the flesh and blood kind of men, were the same all over the world.[1] Reports of strange and different human behaviours were often dismissed as illusory; they were just pirates' tales, or gothic fables. This 18th century sort of scepticism of the very existence of variety in human nature we shall call 'uniformitarianism', following Lovejoy.[2]

In so far as rationalists concede that observed variety is a reality, they believe it is not fundamental. Underlying the appearance of variability is the operation of a hidden order, which explains all the evident variety. This sense of underlying order expresses itself in the belief that specific cases will be explained by general laws, or 'principles'.

Anti-rationalists have the opposite perception of the general state of reality. The world is not a structure; it is a heap. The variety we observe is a reality, not a phantom; it is fundamental, not superficial. Specific realities can be explained only by reference to other specific realities, not by fewer and fewer general laws.

In sympathy with their scepticism about order, anti-rationalists also have a strong sense of the accidental or arbitrary element in the world. Facts are just 'brute facts'. Rationalists, by contrast, are averse to the accidental and arbitrary. They believe there is a reason for things, and they seek to find that reason. So to rationalists everything is intelligible. The world may present us with problems, but never with mysteries. Anything not understood can be 'figured out' and explained in terms of the non-mysterious, the common, the usual.

This rationalist stress on the intelligible, along with the anti-rationalist stress on the unaccountable, underpins another metaphysical contrast between the two. To rationalists the world has an end, or purpose, or 'function'; there is some sense to it. To anti-rationalists the world has no meaning. It is, to adapt Coleridge, an outcast of a blind idiot called Nature. A particular example of this difference between rationalists and anti-rationalists concerns historical change. To rationalists historical change is a meaningful process: the world may be progressing towards perfection, or a classless society, or evolving into higher forms, passing through the four stages, or fulfilling God's plan. To anti-rationalists history is just a random walk.

Epistemology

Rationalists and anti-rationalists also differ regarding the sources, limits and nature of human knowledge. Perhaps most importantly, they differ over the relative significance of the intellect and the senses as sources of human knowledge.

To rationalists the senses are an unreliable source of knowledge; they are misled by appearances.[3] But the intellect, the 'mind's eye', is reliable, as long as the ideas it applies itself to are 'clear and distinct', or 'evident'. 'Clear', 'distinct', 'evident'; these words are the touchstone of rationalist epistemology. Consequently, rationalists believe knowledge begins with 'principles' which are 'so evident that they need only to be understood to be believed' (Descartes, 1985, volume 1, p.145).[4] These evident principles can be manipulated by deductive logic, an operation of the intellect, to demonstrate an indefinitely large range of more particular results.

Although these supposedly evident principles need only to be understood to be believed, rationalists allowed that generally non-philosophers will be unaware of them. This is because these truths are not manifest, or plain to see; they require a well-prepared mind to receive them. So to rationalists truth is to be trapped with ingenuity, rather than casually gathered. As a consequence, rationalists put great stress on method. And since truth is not plain to see, an important part of the right method for hunting out truth was the use of 'hypothesis', 'assumptions' and 'models'.

To anti-rationalists our only source of knowledge is the reports of our senses (where 'senses' include not only the five 'external' senses but also our feelings and appetites). The intellect cannot constitute a fundamental source of knowledge, since the 'mind's eye' can only see what was previously deposited there by the senses. In keeping with this deprecation of the intellect, anti-rationalists are dubious of the value of abstractions and conceptualizations. While rationalists tend to stress the abstractions, conceptualizations and classifications which transform the infinity of particulars into members of homogeneous categories (a tree, a man, a business cycle), the anti-rationalist tends to regard these manipulations of sense reports as necessary evils, at best. At worst, they are merely inferior distortions of sense reports. Leaning away from abstraction, the anti-rationalist is inclined towards induction, the notion that general truths are derived by generalizing, unthinkingly, from repeated sense reports, or 'experience'.

In keeping with their deprecation of the intellect, and their stress on the senses, the anti-rationalists tend to avoid hypotheses, models and systems. In so far as anti-rationalists do tolerate hypotheses, they are inclined to judge them solely by their success in predicting the observed. By contrast, rationalists hold that hypotheses should not be judged solely by their predictive success; there are other criteria of judgement, including analogy with other truths, simplicity, symmetry and 'intelligibility'. Seventeenth century rationalists, for example, rejected the hypothesis of gravitational attraction in spite of its predictive success, on the grounds that it was 'occult' (Malebranche), 'unintelligible' (Fontanelle), or 'supernatural' (Leibniz).

In sympathy with their deprecation of the intellect, anti-rationalists tend to dismiss the role of method in the acquisition of knowledge. To anti-rationalists there is no 'logic of discovery': knowledge is not something which can be produced in any quantity we choose, so long as we 'follow the instructions'. The growth of knowledge cannot be hastened at our pleasure; it has advanced by time-consuming experience and fortuitous accident, and ingenuity cannot quicken this advance. Those truths which are genuinely knowable will 'speak for themselves'; they are apparent. (A good example of this attitude in economics is Richard Jones, who maintained that the only method of answering economic questions is 'to look and see': Jones, 1859, p.568.) And those truths which are not apparent will remain hidden, in spite of all ingenuity. By contrast, rationalists, in keeping with their view that the world was a 'problem' rather than a mystery, were confident that as long as the right method was followed, truth would be flushed out.

Rationalists and anti-rationalists of the 17th and 18th centuries also differed over the role of language in the growth of human knowledge. Both agreed that the existing state of language could be an obstacle to the growth in knowledge. This view was held by a wide range of thinkers, including Descartes, Malebranche, Leibniz, Hobbes, Hume, Locke and Mandeville. The two sides agreed that the obscurity in the meaning of words was a hindrance to thought. But anti-rationalists were additionally dissatisfied with language on the grounds that the few thousand words which make up a language were incapable of capturing the infinite variety of human experience. They also inclined to the old nominalist doctrine that words are a snare, since they invite the 'realization' of mere abstractions. Rationalists were more hopeful about the capabilities of language if properly attended to. Language was, after all, the one feature of the human mind which indisputably distinguished us from the inferior animal world.

These differences between rationalists and anti-rationalists over the source of knowledge clearly have implications for the limits of human knowledge. The anti-rationalist stress on the senses as the source of knowledge suggests that it is only the visible (or 'sensible') which can be known. Therefore the 'underlying causes' of some phenomenon can never be known. By contrast, the rationalist does not see humankind as barred from knowledge of underlying causes by the limits of our senses; the right method will reveal them. Therefore, rationalists tend to seek explanation and cause, while anti-rationalists feel we must be content with mere prediction.

It may appear from the preceding paragraphs that the epistemological differences between rationalists and anti-rationalists can be summarized by saying that rationalists are 'theoretical' in method, while the anti-rationalists are 'anti-theoretical'. This simple summary, however, is made potentially misleading by a treacherous ambiguity in the term 'theoretical'. The term 'theoretical' has both a metaphysical sense and an epistemological sense. A metaphysically theoretical position would amount to a belief in the existence of important general truths (or 'laws'). An epistemologically theoretical position would amount to a stress on the intellect over experience as the source of knowledge. Clearly these two 'theoretical' stances are different. One could believe in the existence of general truths (theoretical in the metaphysical sense), and at the same time believe in the senses as the source of knowledge (anti-theoretical in the epistemological sense). Conversely, one could doubt the existence of general truths, and at the same time stress the intellect as the source of knowledge. The ambiguity in the term 'theoretical' makes for misunderstanding. For example, it is sometimes assumed that economists who are theoretical in the epistemological sense are also theoretical in the metaphysical sense. This need not be so, as a study of 18th century economics will reveal.

Psychology

The contrast between rationalism and its alternative continues into psychological questions. Rationalists believe that humankind is a 'rational' creature, in the sense that we have reasons for doing things. Our actions are not mysterious: they have a rationale, and are explicable in terms of easily comprehensible considerations. This notion lends itself easily to the prosaic vision of human nature which was so popular in the 18th century. It is also strongly suggestive of instrumental rationality, and certain rationalists (Leibniz, Bernoulli, and Maupertuis) did provide important leads on that notion. But it would be wrong to suppose that the rationalists of the 18th century made an assumption of 'instrumental rationality', as modern neoclassicals have.[5] They recognized the concept (although they would have called it 'wisdom' or 'prudence' rather than 'rationality'). But, as with every thinker before the neoclassicals, they never made a tenet of it. Human beings had reasons for doing things, but they did not necessarily have good reasons for doing things.

Rationalists also tended to suppose that man was 'rational' in the sense of being 'thinking', and even 'philosophic'.[6] This thinking characteristic of humankind was supposed to drastically differentiate human beings from animals. Reason was part of the essence of humankind. The idea that being human was inextricably bound up with being rational may have encouraged many rationalists (including Descartes, Leibniz and Hobbes) in their belief that reasoning power is uniformly distributed across humankind.[7]

Anti-rationalists held that humankind is not a thinking (let alone philosophical) creation. The human intellect is not coherent. Rather, in Hume's phrase, the mind is a heap of contradictions. Consequently, the power of the human intellect is limited, and varies so much that the least rational human beings cannot be distinguished from the more rational animals. (Even rationalists who were disdainful of the meagre size of the human intellect, such as Malebranche, abhorred the notion that the mental faculties of human beings were qualitatively comparable to those of animals.)

The psychological contrast between rationalism and anti-rationalism extends to a contrast between an 'inward orientation' and an 'outward orientation'. Rationalism often reflects a pensive, meditative predisposition, where we look upon our mind rather than the world. 'Introspection' is perfectly characteristic of rationalism. So is the stress of rationalists on 'innate ideas'. Anti-rationalism, by contrast, is clearly outward-oriented in its empiricism. In keeping with this contrast, anti-rationalists have pragmatic criteria for success, while rationalists have intellectual criteria. Rationalism seeks to understand the world, while anti-rationalism seeks to change it.

Having examined the metaphysical, epistemological and psychological aspects of rationalism, it is opportune to note that these three aspects meet in the tendency of rationalists to find the intellect everywhere in the world. To rationalists, morals are a matter of reason, beauty is a matter of reason, even sensations are really just 'confused' conceptions. To rationalists the world is a 'reason-infested' place. The anti-rationalist, by contrast, sees sensation and passion everywhere: morals are a matter of feeling, beauty is a matter of pleasure, even concepts are just the 'aftertaste' of sensation. The same contrast between rationalists and anti-rationalists is found in their differing conceptions of belief and theories. Whereas rationalists see beliefs and theories as logical objects, anti-rationalists 'deintellectualize' them. A belief is just a sentiment (belief originally meant 'cherish' in English), or a habit or a rule. A theory is merely a more formal rule or procedure.

These differences over metaphysics, epistemology and psychology are also reflected in a divide over the origins of human culture and technology. Rationalists stress design, foresight and 'genius' in their origins, and anti-rationalists emphasize chance, feeling and tedious experience. This difference is illustrated by their differing doctrines of the origin of language. Eighteenth century rationalists held that language was the product of reason. Anti-rationalists held that language was the product of 'natural' cries (see Berry, 1974; Formigari, 1974).

The purpose of drawing the contrast in the above paragraphs is not to list exhaustively all the properties of 'rationalism'. The only purpose is to highlight the differences relevant to the development of economic thought. Neither is it the ambition of this contrast to reduce the philosophical world to a 'two-party system'. The contrast permits many different positions. Since rationalism and anti-rationalism are clearly complexes, neither need be accepted or rejected as a whole; one is entitled to pick and choose between the elements which make up the complex. One could be a rationalist in some of these divisions and an anti-rationalist in others. As we have already noted, one could adopt rationalist metaphysical tenets without being epistemologically rationalist.

But there is one feature which gives a unity to the doctrines we have classified as rationalist. A thoroughgoing rationalist will be confident that the human mind can fully understand the world, and perhaps even master it. The thoroughgoing anti-rationalist will be doubtful if this world can ever be made our own.

1.2 Rationalism in the historiography of economic thought

Clearly this book proposes to undertake a rationalist history of ideas (see Skinner, 1969, for a critique of such histories). We claim that the history of economics in the 18th century is a meaningful process (of integration), rather than a chaos. We claim that economic thinkers were not directed solely by the unique problems of their own generation and country, but that they struggled with some of the 'timeless' and 'placeless' problems raised by rationalism. And we claim that the subtle analyses of philosophical problems have sometimes touched the thoughts of economists grappling with more mundane questions.

Some historians of economic thought have dismissed the possibility that economic doctrine could be affected by philosophical problems. Schumpeter is a prominent example.[8] His standpoint was probably coloured by his conviction that economic theory was logically autonomous from philosophy, and consequently that any philosophical influences could only have been retarding, not advancing. But given the infant state of economics in the 18th century, why must any philosophical influence have been retarding? An infant science lacks intellectual equipment, and will seek to borrow it from more mature fields. Philosophy is a rich intellectual resource; it has methods of inquiry, it has a stock of suggestive metaphysical doctrines, and it contains theories of psychology. It is plausible that 18th century economics did find nutrient in philosophical doctrines.

Further, the contest between rationalism and anti-rationalism exists outside of the technical debates of philosophers. The divide between rationalism and its critics is an expression of an ancient tension in human thinking, which can be identified to some extent in Classical, Medieval and Modern periods. This tension exists in all thinking ages and in all thinking human beings. It may occur even among deeply religious and anti-scientific ages. It is a tension which has been expressed bitterly in various periods in economics; between Ricardians and their 'historical' adversaries, and by 20th century empiricist critics of both neoclassical and Keynesian economics. The 18th century, the focus of this book, never had such methodological debates, with the exception of some controversies over Physiocracy.

But the absence of debates does not mean there were not differences. Differences existed, and in the following pages we shall attempt to show how the disconcordance of these differences helped form the economics of the Enlightenment.

1.3 An overview of the analysis

The method of analysis will be to select fifteen 18th century thinkers, and to examine how their thought articulated and developed the differences with which this study is concerned. All these thinkers, with one exception, wrote on economic questions. All could be described as philosophers, or, at least, as philosophically conscious. They are well suited to reveal the relevance of the tensions between rationalism and anti-rationalism for the development of economic thought.

The starting point will be the close of the 17th century. At this period economic doctrine consisted of a fund of practical and proverbial wisdom, with a few hints of later growth. This fund was largely deaf to the notion of a market mechanism working systematically in the public interest. From out of these meagre beginnings over the next century classical economics emerged.

A powerful stimulus to the growth of social thought in the following century was supplied by the contrasting world visions of Locke and Leibniz. Locke offered social sciences an anti-rationalist vision, while Leibniz offered a rationalist one. To Leibniz the world was a beneficent order: human nature was uniform, its knowledge came from the intellect, and our pleasures were 'rational'. To Locke the world was an abyss: human beings were wilful, passionate and heterogeneous. These antagonistic visions were briefly given expression within economics by Daniel Bernoulli and Jean-Baptiste Dubos. Dubos, as a follower of John Locke, was hostile to general principles and stressed experience as a teacher. Consequently, the economic method he favoured was factual and specific. Bernoulli, in contrast, as a follower of Leibniz, developed the theory of rational economic man.

As the 18th century progressed, thinkers began to develop hybrids of the pure forms of rationalism and anti-rationalism. Hutcheson and Mandeville combined rationalist metaphysics with the anti-rationalist epistemology and psychology of Locke. They maintained the world was a purposive system, but sought to justify their claims with facts rather than Leibniz's philosophic precepts. Their conception of human nature was 'rationalistic', ahistorical and supranational, and was clearly accommodative of the concept of economic man. But they did not subscribe to *rational* economic man. They held that passion and appetite directed human conduct.

The hybrid position of Hutcheson and Mandeville, rationalist in metaphysics and anti-rationalist in psychology, was strengthened by Hume. In terms of metaphysics, he strengthened their uniformitarianism by arguing that apparent variety in human conduct was only a surface phenomenon, and that underlying human nature was uniform. In terms of psychology, Hume also pressed forward the project of reducing the role of reason in human conduct, and making feeling the measure of all things. He pursued this to the point that reason emerged as a positive hindrance to human survival. At the same time, and in contrast to Hutcheson and Mandeville, Hume shifted social thought towards a more rationalist stance in epistemology. He helped revive theorizing in social science by restoring the empirical credentials of the method of principles.

Condillac and Turgot provided a similar hybrid to Hume; rationalist in metaphysics, anti-rationalist in psychology, but still more distinctly rationalist in epistemology. Condillac effectively strained the empiricism out of Locke, but absorbed his stress on feeling as the measure of all things and combined the two in an economic analysis which anticipated neoclassical theory.

Montesquieu provided a different hybrid again; while he was anti-rationalist in psychology he was also anti-rationalist in metaphysics. In contrast to Condillac, Turgot, Hume and Mandeville, Montesquieu stressed the heterogeneity of humankind. This heterogeneity, apparently hostile to theory, was actually hostile to empiricism since induction by 'tedious experience' becomes unhelpful in a heterogeneous universe. He therefore encouraged more 'analytical' epistemological approaches. This analytical tendency was pursued strongly by Galiani, who was strongly anti-rationalist in metaphysical terms but rationalist in epistemological terms.

These varying attempts at integration of rationalism and anti-rationalism were largely ignored by Physiocracy, which revived some of the most rhapsodic forms of 17th century rationalism. The

Physiocrats' metaphysics and epistemology were in practice strongly rationalist, while human psychology was almost disregarded. They also revived the 'structure of hierarchy' which had been challenged by the alternative notion of a structure of mutual interdependence.

At the close of our period, Smith attempted to integrate these varying responses to rationalism and anti-rationalism. He took a 'judicious' middle path between the two alternatives. He made space for both the hypothetical and the factual, the abstract and the concrete. His doctrines accommodate a general human nature, and give economic man his due, but no more. The notion of a functioning order was accepted, but without flourish. Smith, therefore, constitutes an apogee of the process of synthesis which had been occurring over the previous 50 years.

Notes

1 This shift has a parallel in the abandonment in the 17th century of the Aristotelian dogma that the heavens were the sole location of the perfect, and the earth the location of only the imperfect.

2 Lovejoy went so far as to say '... the central and dominating fact in the intellectual history of Europe for two hundred years - from the late sixteenth to the late eighteenth century' was '... the general attack upon the *differentness* of men ...' (Lovejoy, 1948, p.81). This 'uniformitarianism' was in his judgement 'the first and fundamental principle of this general and pervasive philosophy of the Enlightenment' (Lovejoy, 1948, p.79).

3 The scepticism of testimony which was cultivated by 18th century rationalists served the same purpose as the scepticism of earlier rationalists about the reports of the senses.

4 To be 'distinct' is to be unconfused, to be not mixed up, to be in order. Evidently, the rationalist aversion to disorder in the metaphysical sphere carries over into the epistemological sphere.

5 'Instrumental rationality' means the rationality of successful optimization; for example, the rationality of the consumer who succeeds in maximizing utility, or the firm which succeeds in maximizing profit (see Hargreaves-Heap, 1989, pp. 39-55). 'Instrumental rationality' has nothing to do with the philosophy of 'instrumentalism'.

6 The distinction between 'instrumental rationality' and 'logical rationality' is essentially the philosopher's distinction between 'practical reason' and 'theoretical reason'.

7 Perhaps the notion of the uniformity of human reason across humankind was fostered by the emphasis of rationalists on deductive logic. Deductive logic has an 'all or nothing' quality about it. A defective proof is no proof at all. A defective reason is no reason at all.

8 'Economic analysis has not been shaped at any time by the philosophical opinions that economists happened to have ...' (Schumpeter, 1954a, p.31).

2. The philosophical headwaters: Locke and Leibniz

Classical economics germinated on the margins of the philosophical turbulence of the 17th century. The centre of that turbulence was the New Philosophy of René Descartes and the New Science of Francis Bacon. The radical, renewing outlook of the 'new' philosophy was enormously influential on many thinkers, including John Locke, who 'rejoiced' in reading Descartes (Cranston, 1957, p.100).

But the New Philosophy was fragile. It was run through by a fracture between rationalist and anti-rationalist sentiments. In the last years of the 17th century that fracture received a strong articulation in the contrary philosophies of John Locke (1632-1704) and Gottfried Wilhelm Leibniz (1646-1716). Leibniz produced a powerful rationalist vision of the universe, while Locke advocated an anti-rationalist vision. There is no point in exaggerating the differences between these two thinkers: Leibniz had some definite anti-rationalist sympathies, and Locke had a strong rationalist strain. Yet the contrast between the two survives their similarities.[1]

Their contrasting visions of the social universe had significant consequences for classical economics. At the beginning of the 18th century the scientific analysis of human society was about to intensify. These two influential philosophers offered that analysis quite different pictures of human reality. To Locke the universe was dark, unknowable, fickle, and populated by barely rational human beings. To Leibniz the universe was a perfectly designed whole. It was the 'best of all possible worlds'. It was the solution to a maximization problem.

2.1 Locke on human understanding

The Enlightenment sought to bring light to the world. It is a strong irony that the Enlightenment's preferred philosopher was gripped by images of darkness. To John Locke the human mind is a 'dark room', struggling in an 'Egyptian darkness' (Locke, 1959, IV, iii, 20), lost in a 'huge abyss of ignorance' (Locke, 1959, IV, iii, 24). Locke believed that this huge abyss of human ignorance has several sources; the limits of our rationality, the abuse of words, the limits of our senses, and the complexity of reality.

John Locke had a low estimate of human rationality.[2] The human creature is not philosophical. It has no relish for truth, or 'delight' in knowledge, as Hobbes had supposed (Hobbes, 1962, p.92). On the contrary, the human creature resists and repels truths (Locke, 1959, IV, xx, 12 and 17). To Locke, 'The three great things that governe mankinde are Reason, Passion and Superstition. The first governs a few, the last share the bulk of man kinde and possesse them in their turne' (Dewhurst, 1963, p.158). On another occasion Locke doubted whether reason could even claim a 'few':

> I shall be pardoned for calling it by so harsh a name as madness, where it is considered that opposition to reason deserves that name, and really is madness; and there is scarce a man so free from it, but that if he should always, on all occasions, argue or do as in some cases he constantly does would not be thought fitter for Bedlam than civil conversation. I do not mean here when he is under the power of an unruly passion, but in the steady calm course of life. (Locke, 1959, II, xxxiii, 4)

Locke does allow that humankind has a 'native' faculty of reasoning, given by God, which was exercised to some degree by even infants and savages. He also often entertains the notion that the 'essence' of man is being a rational agent. But almost as often he ponders how one could ever include all the variety of beings which have been considered human under that definition.[3] He remarks 'that there is a difference of degrees in men's understandings, apprehensions, and reasonings, to so great a latitude, that one may, without doing injury to mankind, affirm, that *there is a greater distance between some men and others in this respect, than between some men and some beasts*' (Locke, 1959, IV, xx, 5).[4]

Locke does concede a qualitative difference between the intellects of humans and animals; animals lack the power of abstraction (Locke, 1959, II, xi, 11). But the human power of abstraction is testimony to the mediocrity, not the excellence, of human minds. To Locke abstractions are a crutch; '... if every particular idea that we take in should have a distinct name, names must be endless' (Locke, 1959, II, xi, 9). Abstract ideas merely unburden us of the endless labour of endless names (Locke, 1959, IV, xii, 3). Abstract ideas are only an expedient, they are not the 'foundation of everything we can know in this lower world' (Malebranche, 1980, p.138), as rationalists would assert.[5]

The proof that animals do not have abstractions, says Locke, lies in their lack of signs or words. However, if words are a proof of our power to abstract, they are also one of the largest barriers to human knowledge. Locke's great enemy is the tyranny of words. He carried on a tirade against words throughout Book III of the *Essay Concerning Human Understanding*. Locke's indictment against words included rationalist and anti-rationalist themes. In sympathy with rationalist critics of human language, he complains we use words without 'clear and distinct' meanings, and so our words are so much 'empty sound'. But in sympathy with anti-rationalists, he said the limited stock of words cannot capture the infinite variety of our thoughts and perceptions. (He proposed that in some subjects dictionaries should replace their definitions with pictures of the object denoted.) Also in sympathy with anti-rationalists, he complained that words blind our senses; they 'interpose themselves so much between our understandings, and the truth which it would contemplate and apprehend, that, like the medium through which visible objects pass, the obscurity and disorder do not seldom cast a mist before our eyes ...' (1959, III, ix, 21).

But the 'mist' which words cast before our eyes is not the only reason for our ignorance. Our eyes, our senses, our faculties themselves 'are not fit to penetrate into the internal fabric or *real essences* of bodies' (1959, IV, xii, 11).[6] By the 'real essence' of something (such as gold) Locke meant 'the constitution of the insensible parts of that body, on which those qualities and all other properties of gold depend'. In contrast 'the *nominal essence* of gold is that complex idea the word gold stands for, let it be, for instance, a body yellow, of a certain weight malleable, fusible, and fixed' (1959, III, vi, 2). Locke believed that we are ill-equipped by our senses to peer into the real essence of gold, or any other substance. Therefore we are prevented from learning on what the properties of anything depends. This is a classic empiricist attitude; we can only see the surface, and the hidden underlying causes must remain a matter of 'bare speculation'.

In addition to the poverty of our senses, the limits of our intellect and the delusions of words, Locke believed we are trapped in the abyss of ignorance by the immense variety of the world we live in. It extends in all directions and dimensions and defeats the human mind's attempt to organize it neatly into genus and species (as human language would suggest it could be). Locke was emphatic in stressing the extreme differentness of human beings: in Sparta theft was lawful and customary, Sardinians buried alive decrepit parents, Persians leave corpses to be eaten by dogs, and polygamy 'here is regarded as a right, there as a sin, which in one place is commanded by law, and in another punished by death' (Locke, 1954, p.171).

Owing to the immense variety of nature, Locke with spleen rejects any rationalist programme to attain enlightenment by positing a small set of general principles, and deriving deductively their implications. He remarks by '... how little general maxims, precarious principles, and hypotheses laid down at pleasure, have promoted true knowledge' (Locke, 1959, IV, xii, 12). All principles must be doubtful; we must '... take care that the name of *principles* deceive us not, nor impose on us, by making us receive that for an unquestionable truth, which is really at best but a very doubtful conjecture; such as are most (I had almost said all) of the hypotheses in natural philosophy' (Locke, 1959, IV, xii, 13). In his chapter 'Of Maxims' Locke throws more scorn at deductive reasoning. 'Syllogism, at best, is but the art of fencing with the little knowledge we have, without making any addition to it' (Locke, 1959, IV, xvii, 6). To Locke knowledge 'was founded on particulars' (Locke, 1959, IV, xii, 3), not principles or categories.

Locke evidently rejected the notion of a law-like universe, ruled by a few simple laws. And he had little respect for the human intellect to penetrate the causes of it. These attitudes were articulated in Locke's lifelong study of medicine.

2.2 Locke the medical empirick

Locke was a Bachelor of Medicine, and an 'outstanding' medical practitioner (Cranston), who maintained an interest in medicine throughout his life.[7] From 1652, while an Oxford undergraduate, Locke kept a medical notebook. At Oxford he collected 1,600 specimens from the Botanical Garden for the sake of their medicinal properties. In 1666 he joined Boyle's scientific circle and began collecting weather records, in the hope that it would assist in the 'miasmic' theory of epidemics. (He added to these until the last months of his life.) He made extensive studies of 'iatrochemistry', medical chemistry, physiology, respiration, pharmacology, reproduction, digestion and anatomy. In Oxford he opened a sort of laboratory. Between 1667 and 1672 he was personal physician to Anthony Ashley Cooper, later to become the First Earl of Shaftesbury. In 1674 he graduated as a Bachelor of Medicine and was granted a medical studentship at Christ Church. In the four years 1675-79 he travelled in France and stayed 18 months at Montpellier, the seat of a famous medical school. Between 1679 and 1683 he was a 'diligent student of medicine, rather than a practising physician' (Dewhurst, 1963, p.163). While in exile in Holland between 1683 and 1689 he maintained his medical interests and at one stage lived under the assumed name of Dr Van der Linden, a distinguished medical author whom Locke admired. But in Holland Locke devoted himself to his writings, and his second career as the author of the *Essay Concerning Human Understanding* and the *Two Treatises of Government* began. Locke now only treated friends, but his continued scientific interest in medicine is shown in his surveys of physicians regarding, among other things, the effects of quinine.[8]

The significance of Locke's medical practice was that medicine was the arena of an ancient contest between rationalism and empiricism. This contest dated from Hellenic times and retained life until the close of the 18th century (see King, 1976; King, 1978, chapter 10; and Rousseau, 1972). In antiquity there were essentially two schools of medicine: the Dogmatists and the Empiricists. Dogmatists believed that the basis of scientific medicine was natural philosophy, anatomy and physiology. Empiricists believed 'nature could not be fathomed; hence speculation about these hidden causes, which included elements, humors and pneuma, was useless. They held that medicine had to make do with knowledge of obvious causes, such as hunger, cold and sleep and with clinical experience supported by analogy from similar cases' (Temkin, 1991, p.6).

A Dogmatist would subscribe to a 'theory of medicine' in which truth was supposedly drawn from a set of first principles. In the 17th and early 18th centuries the Galenic system was essentially the orthodox 'theory' of medicine. This system had four 'principles': hot, cold, moist, dry. Incorporated within the Galenic system was the Hippocratic theory of humours. A humour was a liquid or moisture (the word is cognate with 'humid'). The humours included blood, phlegm and bile. There was supposedly a certain right proportion between these humours in the body. A deviation from these proportions would cause illness. For example, the body would attempt to deal with an excess of one humour by 'cooking it': this was a fever. The physician could assist a person with an excess by attempting to remove the excess by 'evacuation', that is, bleeding and emetics.

In the 17th century this Galenic orthodoxy was challenged by modern Empiricists. These included Thomas Sydenham (1624-89), a colleague of John Locke. Sydenham expounds his hostility to medical rationalism in a fragment of an uncompleted book, *De Arte Medica*.

> He that in Physick shall lay downe fundamentall maximes and from thence drawing consequence and raising dispute shall reduce it into the regular forme of a science has indeed done something to enlarge the art of talkeing and perhaps laid a foundation for endless disputes. But if he hopes to bring men by such a system to the knowledg of the infirmities of mens bodys...[he] takes much what a like course with him that should walk up and downe in a thick wood overgrowne with briers and thornes with a designe to take a view and draw a map of the country. (Quoted in Dewhurst, 1966, p.81)

To Sydenham 'true knowledg grew first in the world by experience and rationall operations' (quoted in Dewhurst, 1966, p.81).

Two other aspects of Sydenham's practice put him plainly among the Empiricists. First, his medical interests are entirely pragmatic. He had no use for mere medical learning, or medicine as pure science. Medicine was worthless if it was not useful. Therefore explanations were in themselves redundant; to Sydenham, the question was always 'how?', not 'why?'. In keeping with this precept Sydenham proclaimed, 'I ranke the cooke and Farmer with the Schollar and Philosopher' (quoted in Dewhurst, 1966, p.83). Also in keeping with this precept, Sydenham was a very early advocate of quinine, even though the medical theory of his day could not explain its success. Sydenham's unconcern with explanations can be contrasted with Descartes's research in medicine, which was dominated by his attempt to explain physiology by mechanical principles.

Second, Sydenham was strongly drawn to specific explanations of diseases. There was no single all-explaining theory of illness, as a Galenist would have supposed, but each illness had its own specific explanation. Sydeham's outlook will seem perfectly 'natural' to the 20th century, but it was not considered so in the 17th century.

To John Locke Sydenham was a 'great genius'. Locke appears to have been Sydenham's amanuensis for *Arte Medica*, and several other of his works.[9] Locke's own medical views appear to coincide with Sydeham's. Locke suggests that experience is the best teacher:

> You cannot imagin how far a little observation, carefully made, by a man not tyed up to the four humours; or sal, sulpher and mercury; or to acid and alcili, which has of late prevailed, will carry a man in the curing of diseases, though very stubborn and dangerous, and that with very little and common things, and almost no medicines at all. (Locke, 1976, volume 6, p.145)

Locke held that deductive systems in medicine are worse than useless: 'I have always thought, that laying down, and building upon hypotheses, has been one of the great hindrances of natural knowledge' (Locke, 1976, volume 6, p.144). And like Sydenham, Locke objected to 'general theories' of medicine. They were 'for the most part but a sort of waking dreams ...' (Locke, 1976, volume 4, p.628). Locke deplored how doctors had ignored the specificity of medicine, a very modern view: 'All doctors up to the present century seem to have failed, because in the cure of diseases they have given little thought, or none at all, to the specific nature ... of each disease, and considered solely the bile or phlegm or serum ...' (Dewhurst, 1963, p.136). Locke also faulted medical orthodoxy for seeking cures by pondering the fundamental causes, i.e. by pondering the connection of the 'nominal essence' of the disease (the symptoms) to the real essence of the disease.

> What we know of the works of nature, especially in the constitution of health, and the operations of our own bodies, is only by the sensible effects, but not by any certainty we can have of the tools she uses, or the ways she works by. So that there is nothing left for a physician to do, but to observe well and so by analogy argue to like cases, and thence to make himself rules of practice. (Locke, 1976, volume 4, p.629)

2.3 Locke on the science of mankind

Locke's medical views seem entirely in accord with the anti-rationalist views on the natural science which he expresses in the *Essay Concerning Human Understanding*. However, Locke's treatment of the social sciences is less in accord with these anti-rationalist principles.

This lack of accord is evident at the close of his *Essay* where Locke appeals for human inquiry to turn away from the natural world and towards the human world. Since

> our faculties are not fitted to penetrate into the internal and real fabric and real essences of bodies; but yet plainly discover the being of a God and the knowledge of ourselves, enough to lead us into a full and clear discovery of our duty and great concernment ... our proper employment lies in those enquiries, and in ... the condition of our eternal estate. Hence I think I may conclude, that *morality* is *the proper science and business of mankind in general*. (Locke, 1959, IV, xii, p.350)

What makes Locke's project of a 'science of morality' so anomalous is that it is evidently based on the suggestion that students of a social science are privileged relative to natural science since the 'internal fabric' of the objects of social science *are* fit to be penetrated by our faculties. Human beings *can* see inside the 'human atom', or as Locke puts it, 'Our faculties ... plainly discover ... the knowledge of ourselves'. So while the physical world offers 'bare speculative truth', the human world offers 'right knowledge'.

This position clearly lends itself to the *a priori* method in social science.[10] This position on the privileged status of social science was later used in the 19th century to justify the *a priori* methods of classical political economy (see Cairnes, 1888, p.87). Certainly Locke's own economic analysis is largely *a priori*, with little use of factual material to argue his case. Locke's discussion of economic questions in the chapter on 'Property' in the *Two Treatises of Government* seems entirely *a priori*. In his *Further Considerations Concerning Raising the Value of Money*, he avows that his case is based on 'principles'. He claims these principles 'have their foundation in nature, and are clear: and will be so in all the train of their consequences ...' (Locke, 1823, volume 5, p.134).[11] But Locke's adoption of an *a priori* method in economics is not as inconsistent with his anti-rationalism as it might seem. Locke, as an empiricist, held that all knowledge derived from sense reports. It follows that any barriers to the operation of our senses will prove an impediment to knowledge. But reaching beyond that inference, Locke also seems to have held that it is barriers to the operation of our senses which constitute the *main* impediment to knowledge. If it were not for these barriers there would be no knowledge problem: if we only could 'look', then we could also certainly 'see'. With regard to the social sciences, there are no barriers between ourselves and the operation of our senses. Therefore, knowledge of ourselves is at hand, if we would only look at ourselves and see. So Locke's adoption of the *a priori* method in social affairs is not so much an aberrant elevation of the intellect, but an affirmation of the sufficiency of the senses to supply knowledge if unhindered.

Supposing our faculties can plainly discover knowledge of ourselves, the critic is drawn to ask: does the Lockean philosophy, comprehensively interpreted, imply a 19th century style confidence in theory? Probably not. Recall that Locke's grounds for pessimism about knowledge were four: the unsuitedness of our faculties to penetrate the real essence of things, irrationality, the abuse of words, and the complexity of reality. As we have seen, Locke believed the first difficulty does not apply in social science. Consequently, as we have seen, Locke's pessimism about knowledge in the social sciences is tempered by the relatively privileged state of our faculties in that domain. But the last three grounds for pessimism still apply.

The abuse of words, to be specific, remains a barrier to knowledge in the social sciences. In the *Further Considerations* Locke blames 'hard, obscure and doubtful words' (Locke, 1823, volume 5, p.134) for making the subject of coinage difficult. Locke also attributes fallacies in the matter of coinage to the fact that words, although just labels, have been confused with things. Locke's adversaries in the recoinage debate had advocated a change in mint parities as a remedy for England's financial difficulties. But mint parities, in Locke's view, were just a matter of names. Therefore changing mint parities was just a matter of changing names, and consequently could not change any 'things', such as the value of silver.[12]

Locke's preoccupation with words in the social sciences is also behind his peculiar opinion in the *Essay* that principles of morals may be demonstrated. 'I am bold to think that morality is capable of demonstration, as well as mathematics: since the precise essence of the things moral words stand for may be perfectly known, and so the congruity and incongruity of the things themselves to be certainly discovered' (Locke, 1959, III, xi, 16 and IV, iii, 18). He argues, for example, that 'Where there is no property there is no injustice' is a proposition as demonstrable as any in Euclid. An examination of Locke's proof of this proposition reveals that Locke's 'demonstrable' truths of morality are no more than 'analytic' truths: true by virtue of their meaning. But Locke would not consider demonstrations of moral analytic truths to be of trivial value, since they eliminated purely verbal disputes, and thereby reduced the tyranny of words over the science of morality.

Most importantly, a Lockean pessimism about knowledge in the social sciences would be encouraged by the variety of the world, which Locke so stressed. Such a pessimism seems to have been vindicated by the slow progress in the social sciences. This area has always been dogged by the heterogeneity in its materials. In the light of the great progress in natural sciences since Locke's time, it seems that this heterogeneity in the social world (relative to the natural world) has more than compensated for any supposed special suitability of our faculties to penetrate the social world. It was, however, later argued that it is this same heterogeneity which provides the basis for the economic order. Locke never perceived how this might be. This insight was to come with the work of Mandeville, Montesquieu and Condillac.

2.4 Leibniz and the science of happiness

If Locke was pessimistic, Leibniz was famously optimistic. A discussion of the 'vast genius' of Leibniz (Turgot's words) must begin with Descartes. Descartes (1596-1650) initiated the New Philosophy by doubting all those 'ideas' which were not 'clear and distinct', or (sometimes) 'clear and evident'. His initial project was to derive deductively a system of physics, the natural world, and God from these clear and distinct ideas. This project yielded a highly *a priori* physics, supposedly deducible from indubitable principles, in the manner of Euclid's geometry. It described a physical world ruled by impulse, and without the 'occult' forces of attractions, or any causes of a teleological nature.

In the following generation, Descartes's outlook was developed by Nicolas Malebranche (1638-1715) in *De la Recherche de la Verité*. Malebranche pressed Descartes's doctrine that knowledge began with indubitable 'evidence', a doctrine that was to have so many echoes a century later in Physiocracy.

> First and foremost, the rule we established and proved at the outset of the first book must be remembered, for it is the foundation and first principle of everything we said thereafter. To repeat that rule: *We must give full consent only to those propositions that appear so evidently true that we cannot withhold our consent without feeling inner pain and the secret reproaches* of reason, *i.e. without our knowing clearly that we would make ill use of our freedom were we to withhold our consent.* (Malebranche, 1980, p.409)

Even more importantly Malebranche 'rehabilitated' final causes, which Descartes had deprecated as teleological, and therefore occult. Malebranche used the notion that things can be explained by their purpose to explain the existence of both simplicity and variety in the universe (Malebranche, 1980, p.256).

Leibniz developed a more powerful rationalist vision of the world than either Descartes or Malebranche. This vision was expressed in *Théodicée* of 1710, the 'Leibniz-Clarke Correspondence' of 1717, and the *Nouveaux Essais sur l'Entendement Humain* (a critique of John Locke's *An Essay Concerning Human Understanding*, which was first published in 1765).

Regarding the grounds of knowledge, Leibniz stressed the role of the intellect at the expense of the senses. Leibniz, too, believed that the foundation of knowledge is 'clear and distinct' ideas. Essentially, one has a distinct idea of something if one can define it. If, for example, a gold essayer can state the tests 'which make up the definition of gold', he has a clear idea of gold. If he can successfully identify gold, but cannot state these tests, he does not have a distinct idea of gold. Any ability to recognize something or 'see' something, without the ability to articulate a justification (what one might call 'intuitive' knowledge) is to have only a confused idea.[13]

So to Leibniz to sense something is merely to have a 'confused idea' (Leibniz, 1981, 262). Owing to their confused nature sensations were, by themselves, a weak and unreliable source of knowledge.[14] Induction from experience, for example, could never justify any general proposition without the application of 'universal reason' (Leibniz, 1969, p.130). And a 'king's ransom' could be laid out on experiments, but without the 'art of *using* experiments', it would achieve less than what 'an acute thinker could discover in a moment' (Leibniz, 1981, 455). The art of using experiments, Leibniz believed, requires the hypothetico-deductive method. The success of a hypothesis's predictions in experiment would certainly favour the hypothesis. (Leibniz, 1981, 450). However, in keeping with Leibniz's stress on the intellect, hypotheses should not be judged solely in accord with their success in predicting what our senses observe. There were other intellectual criteria on which hypotheses would be judged. Leibniz, like almost all rationalists, rejected the hypothesis of gravity in spite of its predictive success.

With enough reason Leibniz believed we could dispense entirely with the senses. A superhuman reason could demonstrate all true propositions. But Leibniz, in contrast to Descartes, denied that the laws of nature could be demonstrated merely from considerations of 'absolute necessity'. Matters of 'absolute necessity', according to Leibniz, are those which flow from the Law of Identity and Law of Contradiction. But to Leibniz 'absolute necessity' is the source of only mathematics and geometry. Absolute necessity is not the basis of physical laws: physical laws could have been different from what they are; they are 'contingent'. In fact the entire universe is contingent. It does not have to exist at all.

But Leibniz had a horror of the accidental or arbitrary. The existence of the universe could not have been an accident. The laws of nature could not have been arbitrary. His yearning for a reason behind the state of things was articulated in his 'Principle of Sufficient Reason'. This states that 'nothing happens without a reason why it should be so, rather than otherwise' (Leibniz, 1956, p.16). The Principle of Sufficient Reason expresses a rationalist sentiment: everything has a point.

The Principle of Sufficient Reason would disallow Absolute Space, since Absolute Space requires the Universe to pointlessly possess an arbitrary position. Absolute Time is disallowed on similar grounds. The Principle also forbids Voids, since they are pointless (Leibniz, 1956, p.96). There would be no point in having gaps or jumps in processes, and so the Principle necessitates a Principle of Continuity in Nature.

This Principle of Sufficient Reason lends itself to a faith in a rational and benevolent God directing the universe. It is God's infinite wisdom and benevolence that provides the ultimate reason for everything. For this reason, the laws and the events of the world are not arbitrary (or 'ad hoc') but all devised by God as the best.

Being the best, the laws of nature would not require God's continual intervention, as Leibniz believed gravity required. Being the best, these rational laws will have no pointless complexity or pointless detours. 'The ways of God are the most simple and uniform: for he chooses rules that least restrict one another. They are also the most *productive* in proportion to the *simplicity of the ways and means*. It is as if one said that a certain house was the best that could have been constructed at a certain cost' (Leibniz, 1951, p.257). This optimal simplicity of natural laws reinforced Leibniz's belief that the universe, as a created whole, is a unity in its fundamentals. 'The foundations are everywhere the same; this is a fundamental maxim for me which governs my whole philosophy' (Leibniz, 1981, 490). 'My great principle, as regards natural things, is that of Harlequin, Emperor of the Moon, ... *that it is always and everywhere in all things just like here*. That is, nature is fundamentally uniform ...' (Leibniz, 1981, p.xliv).

Being the best, the laws of nature also obeyed extremum principles. 'There is always a principle of determination in nature which must be sought by maxima and minima; namely, that a maximum effect should take place with a minimum outlay, so to speak' (Leibniz, 1969, p.487). Partly as an outcome of this philosophical principle, Leibniz devised the differential calculus. This was developed in late October/early November 1675 (Edwards, 1979, p.252), and made rapid progress over the next two years. Leibniz applied the technique of maxima and minima in the first paper he published on calculus, *Acta Eridotorum,* in 1684, 'A New Method for Maxima and Minima' (Edwards, 1979, p.258).

To Leibniz, not just the laws of nature, but the whole world was the solution to a maximization problem. And so we arrive at that Leibnizian optimism: that this is the best of all possible worlds.

You may object, however, that we experience the very opposite of this in the world, for often the very worst things happen to the best; innocent beings, not only beasts but men, are struck down and killed, even tortured. In fact, especially if we consider the government of mankind, the world seems rather a kind of confused chaos than something ordained by a supreme wisdom. So it seems at first sight, I admit, but when we look more deeply, the opposite can be established. *A priori* it is obvious from the principles which I have already given that the highest perfection possible is obtained for all things and therefore also for minds. (Leibniz, 1969, p.489)

The notion of the optimum was extended by Leibniz late in his life into the notion of progress (see Leibniz, 1969, paper no. 51). Although at any given point in time the actual world is the best possible world, the best possible world becomes better as time passes! (Leibniz, 1969, p.489). 'At the crown of the universal beauty and perfection of the works of God, we must also recognise that the entire universe is involved in a perpetual and most free progress, so that it is always advancing toward greater culture. Thus a great part of our earth has now received cultivation and will receive it more and more' (Leibniz, 1969, p.491).[15] Human history, in this interpretation, is the best possible path of achieving perfection. If current circumstances sometimes appear bad, it is only a case of stepping back to leap the further. Retrogression is only a means to further progress.

> And though it is true that some sections occasionally revert into wilderness or are destroyed and sink back again, this must be understood in the same sense in which I have just explained the nature of afflictions, namely, that this very destruction and decline lead to a better result, so that we somehow gain through our very loss ... hence progress never comes to an end. (Leibniz, 1969, p.491)

Leibniz applies the logic of optimization to the design of humankind. God could make his creatures any way he liked, but chose them to be the best. He made them naturally healthy. He also gave them reason: 'Reason is a fixed attribute of this kind, associated with the best-known physical species, namely that of humans; reason belongs inalienably to each individual member of the species, although one cannot always be aware of it' (Leibniz, 1981, 310). Leibniz's attitude to human rationality is totally different from Locke's repeated vacillation over human reason. Leibniz, for example, in *Nouveaux Essais sur l'Entendement Humain*, rebukes Locke's suggestion that the intellect of some human beings is so small that it overlaps with animals.

> As for those who lack capacity: there may be fewer of these than you can think, for I believe that good sense together with diligence can achieve any task for which speed is not required. I stipulate good sense because I don't believe that you would require the inmates of Bedlam to engage in the pursuit of truth. Whatever inherent differences there are between our souls (and I believe there

are indeed some), there is no doubt that any soul could achieve as much as any other, though perhaps not quite so quickly, if it were given proper guidance. (Leibniz, 1981, 511)

Leibniz also hints at the notion of a human, maximizing decision maker choosing optimally between alternatives.

> ... since there are often more than two ways which a man may take; we may therefore ... compare the soul to a force, which has at one and the same time a tendency many ways, but acts on that part only where it finds the greatest ease, or the least resistance. For example: air strongly impressed in a glass receiver, will break the glass to get out. It presses upon every part, but at last makes its way where the glass is weakest. (Leibniz, 1956, p.131)

The notion of instrumental rationality is latent here. This is not to say that Leibniz believed that human beings were in fact instrumentally rational (see, for example, Leibniz, 1981, 512). But he had a clear conception of what he called the 'science of happiness' (or 'wisdom'), and was optimistic about the possibility of discoveries in this science.

Locke's treatment of instrumental rationality has similarities and differences from Leibniz. Locke states that 'every man is put under a necessity, by his constitution as an intelligent being, to be determined in willing by his own thought and judgement what is best for him to do' (Locke, 1959, II, xxi, 49). There is nothing Leibniz would disagree with here.[16] It is not far from the modern neoclassical notion of a person maximising utility.

Yet Locke is troubled much more than Leibniz by the thought that man, nevertheless, does not choose what is best for him: '... since men are always ... in earnest in matters of happiness and misery the question still remains, *How men often come to prefer the worse to the better; and to chuse that which, by their own confession, has made them miserable?*' (Locke, 1959, II, xxi, 37, p.378). How is it that men so often 'abandon themselves to the brutish, vile irrational actions during the whole current of a wild and dissolute life?' (Locke, 1959, II, p.380). How is it that men are deficient in wisdom and prudence, or what we would call 'instrumental rationality'? In Chapter xxi of Book II of the *Essay* he explains the choice of misery and irrational actions by reference to 'the weak and narrow constitution of our minds'. He lays particular stress on this weak and narrow constitution making for irrational decisions in an intertemporal context. He says that with regard to the present 'a man never chooses amiss; he knows what best pleases him' (Locke, 1959, II, xxi, 60). But with respect to intertemporal decisions we do choose amiss.

Locke and Leibniz also differed over the extent of the domains of reason and passion. According to Leibniz 'the pleasures of sense are reducible to intellectual pleasures, known confusedly'. The beauty of music, for example, consists 'only in the agreement of numbers and in the counting ... of the beats' (Leibniz, 1969, p.641). Locke reversed the relative pre-eminence of reason and passion; to Locke many intellectual judgements were merely the offspring of appetite. 'The mind has a different relish, as well as the palate ... Hence it was, I think, that the philosophers of old did in vain enquire, whether *summum bonum* consisted in riches, or bodily delights, or virtue, or contemplation: and they might have as reasonably disputed, whether the best relish were to be found in apples, plums, or nuts, and have divided themselves into sects upon it' (Locke, 1959, II, xxi, 56). Here Locke adopts a subjectivist (or emotivist) theory of the good. Locke had given a start to the anti-rationalist project to remove reason as the arbiter in all human affairs.

Yet Locke was not entirely exempt from the rationalist tendency to intellectualize the passions. Our very preference for present pleasure over future pleasure is seen by Locke to be a consequence of weak-mindedness:

> when we compare present pleasure or pain with future, (which is usually the case in most important determinations of the will,) we often make wrong judgements in them; ... Thus most men, like spendthrift heirs, are apt to judge a little in hand better than a great deal to come; .... But this is a wrong judgement everyone must allow, ... Were the pleasure of drinking accompanied, the very moment a man takes off his glass, with that sick stomach and aching head which, in some men, are sure to follow not many hours after, I think nobody whatever pleasure he had in his cups, would, on these conditions, ever let wine touch his lips; which yet he daily swallows, and the evil side comes to be chosen only by the fallacy of a little difference in time. (Locke, 1959, II, xxi, 65)

Locke's contention that time preference is irrational is followed by many later economists: it is reflected in Smith's strictures on the prodigal. Whether this judgement is correct is immaterial here, the important point is that Locke analysed this preference as an intellectual failing. It indicates that Locke had left unfinished the anti-rationalist project of removing reason as the arbiter of human affairs.

2.5 Conclusion

So, in summary, what are the bequests of Locke and Leibniz to classical economics? With regard to psychology, Locke's writings are hostile to the notion of man being rational in the instrumental sense. Man is wilful and rash. Reason could not claim to rule in human values either, since values were just a matter of passion.

Epistemologically, Locke's philosophy of science proved a rather thin soil for the growth of the science of man. His empiricism tended to be a rather facile 'look and see' empiricism, which glided by the problems of deriving truth from the chaos of experience. His faith in the power of looking and seeing implicitly countenanced the looking at ones own feelings and thoughts (i.e. introspection), and thereby unwittingly encouraged an *a priori* approach to social issues.

Locke's preoccupation with words only served to deflect attention away from experience. His belief that the knowledge problem was tied up with words suggested to his 18th century French developers that words will provide the answer to the knowledge problem. Words, instead of being the problem, would be the solution. Locke's stress on analytic truths had the same effect of diverting the attention of his followers away from experience. His conviction that words were an obstacle to knowledge did, however, promote developments in monetary theory. His claim that in monetary affairs words had been confused with things encouraged the notion of money neutrality. If money is treated as a name or sign, then the notion of words as a 'mist' and money as a 'veil' are highly cognate. Hume, for example, judged money to be a 'sign' and concluded, on the basis of nominalist thinking, that changes in the quantity of money would not change any real thing. We see this logic even more explicitly in Galiani in his 1751 analysis of increases in the money supply: an increase in the money supply 'does not produce any change in things, but in names' (quoted in Cesarano, 1976, p.393).

Metaphysically, Locke seems oblivious to the notion of natural laws, which barely receive a mention in his *Essay*. His empiricism is one almost without laws: a chaotic empiricism; an empiricism full of particulars, but of few generals. The *Essay* emphasizes diversity, but provides little hint of a law-like social universe, no hint of history and progression or evolution.

The atmosphere of Locke's writings is pessimistic. Locke drew a world which was irrational, disjointed and gloomy, a world in which human beings are trapped by their own passions and limitations in an Egyptian darkness.

Leibniz, in contrast, drew a world which was rational, homogeneous and hopeful. Whereas, to Locke the mind was a dark room, to Leibniz it was a mirror. To Locke human society is a chaotic irregularity; to Leibniz life is the same here, in Egypt and on the moon. To Locke we all, at some stage in our life, belong in Bedlam, but to Leibniz we smoothly follow the path of the 'greatest ease'.

Notes

1 Stark advances the opposite viewpoint. He stresses the similarity rather than the differences between Locke and Leibniz. 'Leibniz developed a theory of individual action and social ethics closely akin to that propounded at the same time by John Locke. Sociology is the field where the great antagonists meet ... about the social aspect of man and mankind they thought almost alike. This is the deeper reason for the union of their ideas which is visible in classical economics from Adam Smith to Frederic Bastiat' (Stark, 1943, p.43).

2 In the *Essay* Locke devotes an entire chapter to explaining the many causes of human error (Locke, 1959, IV, xx).

3 'To be rational is so glorious a thing that two-legged creatures generally content themselves with the title' (Locke quoted in Cranston, 1957, p.466). Locke's hesitation about the essence of man is seen further in Book III, xi, 20 of the *Essay*.

4 Our italics.

5 Locke's claim corresponds to Hayek's and Condillac's thesis that abstract ideas are the necessary consequence of the limits of our mind.

6 Our italics

7 Locke's medical career has been copiously researched by Dewhurst (1963) and Romanell (1984).

8 Dewhurst credits Locke with the 'first detailed account' of 'suppurating hydatid abscess of the liver' (Dewhurst, 1963, p.37), the first diagnosis of trigeminal neuralgia (Cranston, 1957, p.173), and 'the first description of onychogryphosis' (Dewhurst, 1963).

9 Dewhurst ascribes the authorship of *Arte Medica* to Sydenham. Romanell (1984) defends the traditional attribution of the authorship to Locke. Both agree the manuscript is in Locke's hand.

10 In Schumpeter's judgement Locke preserved in economic and political theory the Aristotelian method he destroyed in epistemology (Schumpeter, 1954a, p.117). Schumpeter designates Locke in economic issues a 'Protestant Scholastic'. In a similar vein, Mini (1974) maintains that Locke's rationalist element was conducive to the development of the theoretical method of classical economics.

11 It is appropriate to note here that Locke's posthumously published *Conduct of the Understanding* is far more 'rationalistic' in tone than the *Essay*. For example, 'Most of the difficulties that come in our way. when well considered and traced, lead us to some

proposition, which, known to be true, clears the doubt, and gives easy solution to the question' (Locke, 1823, volume 3, p.283). Locke also praises the 'fundamental truth', 'rich in store', which 'lie at the bottom, the basis upon which a great many others rest' (Locke, 1823, volume 3, p.282).

12 Hutcheson adopted as a 'fundamental maxim' the Lockean doctrine that the value of metals is not changed by their names (Taylor, 1965, p. 76).

13 Leibniz's distinction between confused and distinct ideas is parallel to Hayek's distinction between being able to recognize truth and being able to prove it.

14 But Leibniz allows that in some situations the senses do provide important knowledge. Leibniz criticizes Descartes for neglecting experience in his physical hypotheses (Leibniz, 1969, p.272). Leibniz also judged Bacon's *Novum Organum* to be 'brilliant' (Leibniz, 1969, p.89).

15 The paper from which this quotation was drawn was only published in 1840.

16 Leibniz might have scrupled over the word 'necessity'. No choice is necessary, to Leibniz, even if the choice is certain. God can choose what is not good, although it is certain that God will choose only what is good. Locke says 'God himself *cannot* choose what is not good' (Locke, 1959, II, xxi, 50). Stark expands on this difference between the two philosophers (1943, p.44).

3. The divergent streams: Dubos, Bernoulli and Maupertuis

The last chapter contrasted the rationalism of Leibniz with the anti-rationalism of Locke. We now pursue this contrast in the generation which followed. In that generation Leibniz's science found brilliant adherents among members of the Bernoulli family, including Daniel Bernoulli. Locke's philosophical doctrines also found many admirers. Among these were Jean-Baptiste Dubos, a historian, critic, and political economist. From Pierre-Louis Maupertuis, Leibniz and Locke won a peculiar double loyalty. All three, Dubos, Bernoulli and Maupertuis, made brief forays into economic questions. These writings clearly indicate the tendency of rationalism and anti-rationalism to foster very different kinds of economics.

3.1 Dubos and the misrule of reason

Jean-Baptiste Dubos (1670-1742) was an important articulator of Lockean philosophy in early 18th century France (see Hutchison, 1991). Dubos was a savant abbé who composed chronicles, philosophized taste, and practised secret diplomacy. A sociable erudite with a liking for travel, he befriended several leading elements of the philosophic world, including John Locke.

In July 1698, already competent in English, Dubos crossed the Channel equipped with letters of recommendation to John Locke. Locke, perhaps impressed by these letters, sought out Dubos in his London lodgings, and welcomed him 'most cordially' (Bonno, 1950, p.484). Over the next two months Dubos made the acquaintance of various scientific notables in London. At the Royal Society he inspected William Petty's catamaran-like sailing boat. In London he read Petty's *Political Arithmetic* and Locke's *Further Considerations Concerning Raising the Value of Money* (Lombard, 1969, p.76). On his return to France, Dubos was accompanied by Locke to his ship.

The friendship of Locke and Dubos was maintained by a literary correspondence. Dubos alerted Locke to new books, especially ones on exploration and travel: Captain Pelsart in New Guinea, buccaneers in the Antilles, Jesuits in China, missionaries in Persia, and the discoveries of William Dampier, whom he had met in London. These books are often praised by Dubos as full of curious things.[1] Locke's 'long letters' (Bonno, 1950, p.490) to Dubos have been lost, but they included parts of the 1700 French translation of the *Essay* (Bonno, 1950, p.519).

Many of Dubos's writings display the influence of Locke. Dubos's earliest political treatise is an advocacy of a constitutional monarchy. The *Traité sur la Succession à la Couronne* of 1718 claimed that monarchy was instituted, not by God, but by a 'human pact' between the sovereign and the people, such that the people can alter the terms of it when they so wish (Kaiser, 1989). There is nothing essential here which John Locke would disagree with.[2]

Locke's influence is also plain in the book which made Dubos's reputation: the *Réflexions Critiques sur la Poésie et sur la Peinture,* published in 1719. This book went through seven editions and several translations; it was commended by Hume as 'ingenious' and borrowed from extensively by Condillac in his *Essai sur l'Origine des Connaissances Humaines*. Smith owned a copy, and refers to Dubos in the *Theory Of Moral Sentiments*, and in his *Lectures on Rhetoric and Belles Lettres*. It is largely on the basis of the *Réflexions* that the longest study of Dubos was entitled, *The Abbé Du Bos. A Pioneer of Modern Thought* (Lombard, 1969).

The *Réflexions* is a treatise on the appreciation of poetry and painting. But from the vantage of this polite subject Dubos seems to throw down a challenge to all the epistemological assumptions of French rationalism. He is forcefully empiricist, subjectivist and relativist. He repudiates the method of principles and proof. He appears to reject the whole civilizing presumption of reason, and identifies it with barbarism. 'I will content myself by saying that the philosophic mind which renders men so reasonable, and so to speak, *so rational,* will soon do to a large part of Europe what Goths and Vandals did another time, assuming it continues to make the same progress that it has made over the last seventy years' (Dubos, 1967, part II, section xxxiii).

How is it that rationalism could ransack a civilization? By neglecting the realities of human psychology. Humankind, said Dubos, is an active, not a philosophic, species; it is one which wants to be excited rather than enlightened. Man is a creature which can be moved, but follows reasons with difficulty and unreliable competency: 'one is mistaken all the time when behaving as a philosopher, that is to say, by establishing general principles, and drawing from these principles a succession of conclusions ...' (Dubos, 1967, part II, section xxiii). The philosophical method of principles and proof leads only to a blind attachment to authority, the discord of rival 'orthodoxies', and the verbal swordplay, wrangling and disputing which so repelled Locke and Sydenham.

Advances in knowledge come only from experience:

> The older men grow, and the more their reasoning is perfected, the less faith they have in all philosophical reasonings; and the more trust they have in feeling and practice. Experience has shown them that one is rarely tricked by the distinct report of one's senses, and that the habit of reasoning and judging on these reports leads to a simple and reliable practice. (Dubos, 1967, part II, section xxiii)

Dubos made his case for experience by reference to the invention of locks, windmills, watermills, clocks, gunpowder, compass, spectacles and printing. All these, he said, were discovered by ordinary people in everyday situations, not philosophers. 'They argue about the first inventor of printing, but no one gives this honour to a philosopher' (Dubos, 1967, part II, section xxxiii). This sentiment is entirely in sympathy with Locke and Sydenham's esteem of the 'illiterate and contemned mechanic' who has provided the world with the 'useful arts' (Locke, 1959, III, x, 9).

The most valuable experience is new experience, and inevitably this is largely chance experience. Given this, Dubos believed the growth of knowledge cannot be rushed. Contrary to the rationalist contention, there is no algorithm or 'right method' for producing new knowledge, there is no 'logic of discovery'. Consequently, Dubos rejected the notion of a 'methodological revolution' in the 17th century, whether it be quantitative, mathematical *or* empirical. No new philosophic method has accounted for the growth of knowledge in modern times; there has been no 'scientific revolution' distinguishing Moderns from the Ancients; our methods of reasoning are no better than the Ancients.

In order to prove that we reason better than the Ancients, it would be necessary to show that it is to sound reasoning, and not to chance or fortuitous experience, that we owe the knowledge that we possess and they did not. But far from being able to show that we owe these new discoveries to philosophers who reached the most important natural truths, by methodical researches or by the art, which is so praised, of linking conclusions together, one can prove the contrary. One can show that these inventions and original discoveries, so to speak, are due solely to chance .... (Dubos, 1967, part II, section xxxiii)

The Moderns may have made more discoveries, but only due to chance observation and not to reason. For example, the Moderns know how to treat malarial fever more effectively than the Ancients, but only thanks to the fortuitous discovery of quinine, whose properties had been explored by empiricist physicians (such as Sydenham and Locke). In defiance of the pretensions of the New Science, Dubos held the Ancients in high regard. They were closer to the truth than the Moderns allowed: Aristarchus had maintained the heliocentric system, and Hippocrates had 'vaguely' guessed the circulation of blood.

Dubos's elevation of observation and experience over the intellect had consequences which extended beyond the growth of scientific knowledge; it also yielded a new criterion for aesthetic judgement, the ultimate purpose of the *Réflexions*. In defiance of Cartesian precepts, Dubos claimed reason is not the criterion for judging art; our senses are. We have a 'sixth sense' of beauty. This clearly encouraged the notion that beauty is subjective and relative. This doctrine also had a broader significance: by 'sensualizing' beauty Dubos was pursuing the anti-rationalist drive to unseat reason from its position of power, as the dictator and judge of every aspect of human life. This campaign to scour the world of the 'infestation of reason', already begun by Locke, was later carried on by Hutcheson into moral questions, and by Hume into almost everything.

Dubos's elevation of the senses against the intellect also encouraged a new respect for imagination, since our senses constitute the building blocks of the imagination. By praising our senses Dubos is not only rehabilitating feeling against reason, but also imagination against reason, and the scorn of rationalists such as Malebranche. This resurrection of the imagination appears to have been influential on Hume and Smith. The imagination is a central feature of Hume's account of the human mind, and Smith's analysis of science. The imagination also suggested the 'sympathetic imagination', the imagining that you were somebody you were not, something which is obviously important in Smith's theory of moral judgements.

3.2 Dubos and political arithmetic

Dubos's method, his elevation of practical experience over speculative reason, of sense over intellect, and the relative over the absolute, would have consequences if applied to economic problems. This may be partly seen in his one work expressly concerned with economic questions: his *Les Intérêts de l'Angleterre Malentendus Dans la Guerre Présente* (1703). This was a widely issued work, reprinted twelve times within 1704, and translated into two languages. Its supposition about the balance of trade between England and Scotland is referred to by David Hume in his essay of 1754, 'Of the Balance of Trade' (Hume, 1987, p.314).

Les Intérêts was occasioned by the conflict between England and France in the War of Spanish Succession. It was an attempt to persuade the English that their foreign policy was economically irrational. Dubos's analysis of England's economic interest is barely coloured by any general principles; rather it is an appeal to the specific case, practical lessons and fact. Dubos's chief resource in this appeal were the English political arithmeticians, whose figures on excise revenue and coinage he quotes in detail. His sources include William Petty, Josiah Child and Charles Davenant, whose *An Essay on the Ways and Means of Supplying the Present War* Locke had sent Dubos, on his request, in 1702.[3] Indeed, Dubos wrote the preface of the anonymously issued *Les Intérêts* so as to suggest Josiah Child was the author.

What Dubos found so congenial about the political arithmeticians was their highly specific vision of reality. There is little indication, for example, that their leading member, William Petty (1623-87), saw the world as a matter of general principles. Petty was metaphysically an anti-rationalist. His writings are a miscellany of ideas and observations, speculations and queries. He infrequently generalized, he rarely abstracted, and rarely made explicit his premises. His more general claims (such as they are) seem barely to reach beyond proverbial wisdom. Petty's world is one of particulars, especially particular policy questions. And his concern for policy questions yielded his innovative and celebrated quantitative method. Petty believed that the calculation of specific factual magnitudes was *necessary* to answer particular policy questions; abstract general principles could not suffice. On one occasion Petty compared the attempts of government to promote commerce without knowledge of particulars to the attempts of a gambler to obtain better numbers at dice by throwing them harder; both efforts were perfectly useless (Petty, 1899, volume 1, p.53). The specific contribution of political arithmetic to policy, therefore, was that it supplied a technique of capturing the full specificity of situations, the technique of quantification. Mere 'comparative words' could not fully capture the specificity and should therefore be avoided.

This quantitative orientation of the political arithmeticians also gave their work a highly empirical flavour. Petty prefaced his *Political Arithmetic* with a statement that seems almost to amount to an empiricist manifesto: '... instead of using only comparative and superlative Words, and intellectual Arguments, I ... express myself in Terms of *Number, Weight* or *Measure*; to use only Arguments of Sense, and to consider only such Causes, as have visible Foundations in Nature ...' (Petty, 1899, volume 1, p.244).

It is true, as several critics have stressed, that Petty makes no attempt to infer generalizations or 'empirical laws' from his factual data (Aspromourgos 1986, p.40; Schumpeter, 1954a, p.211; Endres, 1985). Schumpeter goes so far as to describe Petty as 'first and last a theorist' (Schumpeter, 1954a, p.211). Schumpeter is exaggerating. The fact that Petty was not inductive does not make him anti-empirical. He did not seek generalizations by induction because he did not expect such generalizations to exist.[4] In the 'metaphysical' sense Petty was *anti*-theoretical: he did not believe the world was a matter of general principles. There is, however, one sense in which he may be described as theoretical in approach: he sought explanation. Petty was interested in 'why?' and not merely 'how?'.

Petty's own medical practice is supportive of this interpretation of his methodology as metaphysically and epistemologically anti-rationalist, but with a rationalist concern to obtain the underlying causes of things.[5] Medicine, as we have seen, had been something of a battleground between rationalism and anti-rationalism. In keeping with empiricists Petty emphasized a doctor's personal experience over 'lame words' (Petty, 1927, p.176). Yet he urges 'The physician must be a philosopher, skilled at large in the phenomena of nature; must understand the Greek tongue, be well read in good authors, ...' (Petty, 1808, volume 6, p.8). Further, Petty's medical practice is not merely pragmatic, it is not interested merely in the 'how' of things; it is concerned with the scientific fundamentals of bodily function, especially anatomy. Anatomy, says Petty, is the 'best foundation' of the study of the Body Natural; to practise without knowing the '*Symmetry*, *Fabrick* and *Proportion* of it, is as *casual* as the practice of Old-women and Empyricks' (Petty, 1899, volume 1, p.129). This stress on anatomy as a necessary foundation for medical practice sharply distinguished Petty from some empiricists, including Sydenham. Yet Petty could not remotely be described as a Galenic dogmatist. Petty's anatomy was a Baconian New Science, seeking explanation by direct observation of the relevant particulars.[6]

So it makes sense that Dubos found inspiration for his economics in the political arithmeticians, who shared his stress on specifics and his hostility to general principles. However, Dubos had more grounds than the political arithmeticians for being drawn to a vision of reality that was specific. Dubos's vision of humankind was richer than the narrowly 'material' outlook of many political arithmeticians. Dubos allowed 'moral' factors a role. For example, he stressed the differences between national characters, even over fundamentals. According to Dubos, for example, the English have little aversion to death (Dubos, 1704, pp.54,55).[7] (Smith contrasts the character of Italians and English on the basis of a reference to Dubos: Smith, 1982b, p.207.) And according to Dubos the English, in contrast to the Dutch, despise economy in expenditure. Dubos's outlook, by emphasizing feeling, tradition, time and place, could have lead to a political economy far richer than that of the political arithmeticians. It would also have produced an economics very different from that of classical economics. It may have led to a culture-specific economics, in which the fundamentals are found in diversity instead of unity.

Some raw materials for the development of a culture-specific economics were available early in the 18th century. Petty had already pointed to the economic vigour of the religiously heterodox portion of society (Petty, 1899, volume 1, p.263). Another source of materials were social values: 'honour' for example, which attracted so much interest in the 18th century.[8] Montesquieu had made honour the basis of monarchy. In 1741 Hume suggested that the economic dynamism (or lethargy) of any society could be explained by the degree to which trade was honoured in that society (Hume, 1987, p.93). At the time of Dubos's death in 1742 a culture-specific political economy may have seemed just as possible as the culture-general classical economics that was about to emerge.

How might one summarize Dubos's contribution? Above all else, he challenged the pretension of reason to an exclusive domain over human affairs. Specifically, he helped foster a respect for Lockean empiricism in France. Long before Locke received the praise of Voltaire in the *Lettres Philosophiques* (Voltaire, 1943, pp.39-44), Dubos had argued the Lockean notion that experience is the source of all useful knowledge. This became a maxim repeated *ad nauseam* by Enlightenment notables (e.g. D'Alembert, Turgot, Condillac, Diderot).

Dubos also nurtured the idea of a useful 'imagination', which was so fertile in Hume and Smith's epistemology and ethics. Further, by removing beauty from the rule of reason, he showed the way for Hutcheson and Hume to do the same in morals, and by suggestion all judgements. Thus, perhaps most importantly of all, Dubos's stress on the subjectivity and relativity of things was highly congenial to a utility theory of value, and contrary to any 'absolute' theory of value. The first subjectivist theory of value, pursued with any tenacity, appeared in 1751 in Galiani's *Della Moneta*. The essential relativity of value, its nature as an expression of the difference between the personal satisfactions that an individual obtains from two goods, and the highly variable nature of those satisfactions, are all pressed by Galiani. Galiani claimed a great novelty in his theory (Galiani, 1955, p.48). This claim was overstated. Nevertheless, his doctrine would be impossible under the old rationalist hegemony. The early dissenters from rationalism, such as Dubos, had made subjectivist theories of value possible.

But not all of Dubos's challenges to rationalism thrived. His hostility to general principles was largely a failure, especially in economics. If he succeeded in bringing the epistemology of John Locke to France, his attempt to import the method of Josiah Child and William Petty fizzled. Economic analysis was increasingly to 'behave as a philosopher'; to establish general principles, and draw from them a succession of conclusions. And although Dubos's highly specific vision of social reality stimulated Montesquieu's sociology, it had little influence on the rapid development of economics after 1750. The classical economics that was to emerge in the generation after his death was general and supranational.

3.3 Daniel Bernoulli and utility-maximizing man

The most immediately fruitful bequest of Leibniz's rationalism to social science lay in the study of human conduct. Leibniz had held hopes for the development of the analysis of rational decision making, or in his phrase 'the science of happiness'. And he had left his followers one technique magnificently adapted to its analysis: the calculus of maximization. In the 30 years following his death, some first steps were taken in this new 'science'. In the generation following Leibniz, the generation of Daniel Bernoulli and Pierre-Louis Maupertuis, the seeds of neoclassical utility maximization were planted .

Daniel Bernoulli lived in an intellectual milieu dominated by Leibniz. The father and uncle of Daniel Bernoulli, Johann I Bernoulli (1667-1748) and Jakob I Bernoulli (1654-1705), were the chief developers of the strictly scientific element in Leibniz's vision. From 1687 the two brothers were engrossed in infinitesimal calculus: they were 'the first to achieve a full understanding of Leibniz's abbreviated presentation of differential calculus' (Fellman and Fleckstein, 1970). In 1693 Johann I began a correspondence with Leibniz, the most extensive correspondence of the latter. The result of this was that Johann I became an advocate of Leibnizian (i.e. non-Newtonian) physics (Whewell, 1967, p.69). Johann's older brother Jakob I also contributed to the new calculus: he was the first to deploy the term 'integral' in its present mathematical sense.

Jakob I Bernoulli was also interested in probability. At the time of his death in 1705 his celebrated *Ars Conjecturi* remained unpublished.[9] But the subject of probability had already been given prominence by Pierre Rémond de Montmort (1678-1719). Montmort had absorbed Cartesian physics under the tutelage of Malebranche and his circle, but devoted his research to games of chance. The publication of his *Essai d'Analyse sur les Jeux de Hasard* in 1708 prompted a correspondence with a nephew of Jakob I Bernoulli, Nikolaus I Bernoulli. (Nikolaus I had a little earlier defended a thesis that had won the praise of Leibniz: 'On utilising the art of conjecture in juristic matters'. This had applied probability to a number of legal problems, including debt repayment. See Maistrov, 1974, p.57.) The correspondence of Montmort and Nikolaus I Bernoulli of 1710-12 was published in the second edition of the *Essai*. This edition introduced what later became known as the St Petersburg Paradox. The 'solution' to the Paradox was advanced independently by Daniel Bernoulli and Gabriel Cramer. Their solutions were the occasion of the first formal analysis of utility maximization.

Gabriel Cramer (1704-52), of Cramer's rule fame, was a Genevan mathematician and editor of the correspondence of Johann I Bernoulli and Leibniz. Between 1727 and 1729 Cramer spent five months in Basel with Johann I Bernoulli and Daniel Bernoulli, and it was perhaps in this period that Nikolaus introduced this problem to him. Cramer's solution was presented in a letter of 1728. He suggests that the expectation of the square root of wealth, rather than the expectation of wealth, is what people maximize. This suggestion is justified on the grounds that 'while it is true that 100 millions yield more satisfaction than do 10 millions, they do not give 10 times as much' (Bernoulli, 1954, p.34). In other words, diminishing marginal utility.

Independently of Gabriel Cramer, Daniel Bernoulli (1700-82) had presented a superior solution. This solution displayed the rationalistic temper characteristic of much of his work. Daniel Bernoulli's early studies in medicine were, in keeping with his rationalist orientation, overwhelmingly concerned with the basic science of the body, not with medicine as the 'art of curing'. He, like Descartes, sought a mechanical understanding of physiology. He later produced treatises on the mechanical aspects of breathing, the mechanical work of the heart, and a mechanical theory of muscular contraction. In physics Daniel remained within the rationalist sphere, seeking an explanation of gravitation in terms of the rotation of 'subtle matter'.

In 1725 Bernoulli accepted a position in mathematics at the Imperial Academy of Sciences of St Petersburg, which had been recently established under the auspices of Leibniz. In 1728 the Academy began a journal, the *Transactions of the Academy of St Petersburg*, which was strongly Leibnizian in tone, if we may judge from the fact that the first issue contained three Leibnizian memoirs (Whewell, 1967, p.69).

It was in the *Transactions* that Bernoulli published his paper of 1731, 'Exposition of a New Theory on the Measurement of Risk'.[10] Bernoulli writes there of Cramer's theory, 'I have found his theory so similar to mine that it seems miraculous that we independently reached such close agreement on this sort of subject'. But Bernoulli's paper involves a rather more expansive treatment of the problem than Cramer's. It is technically superior, being based on the new Leibnizian differential calculus, a technique Cramer 'never accepted or mastered' (Jones, 1970). Bernoulli's paper displays his facility in the new calculus; it supposes $dy = b\ dx/x$, where y is utility and x is wealth, and he obtains by integration the utility function, $y = b\ log\ x/\alpha$. Further, the St Petersburg Paradox is treated by Bernoulli as just one manifestation of a more general thesis of maximizing behaviour: that people conduct themselves so as to secure the greatest expected utility. Samuelson justly writes, 'A 1954 or 1977 reader of Bernoulli's 1738 paper will be struck by its modernity of tone' (1977, p.39). Bernoulli provided the world with a formal theory of rational choice almost 150 years before Jevons, in the years Vitus Behring discovered Behring Strait and Johann Sebastian Bach composed the *St Matthew Passion*.

3.4 Maupertuis and cost-minimizing nature

An indication of the broader potential of rational choice theory was provided by a pupil of Johann I Bernoulli, Pierre-Louis Moreau de Maupertuis (1698-1759). Maupertuis was one of the most fertile minds of the 18th century: he had an invention, a plasticity, a restlessness, which impelled him to leap between geography, biology, physics, linguistics, morals and music. (See Brunet, 1929, and Beeson, 1992, for studies of his work.) Although a pupil of Johann I Bernoulli, his wandering mind led him far beyond the boundaries of rationalist precepts. Maupertuis managed an allegiance to both Leibniz and Locke.

Epistemologically, Maupertuis was an empiricist. So in epistemological terms he was far closer to Locke or Dubos than the continental rationalists. As an empiricist, Maupertuis regarded the senses as the source of knowledge. As an empiricist, he was antagonistic to systems and theories: 'Systems are real misfortunes for the progress of science' (Maupertuis, 1965, volume 2, p.257). And, the critical test of empiricism, he was scornful of theoretical medicine: 'Medicine is far from being able to deduce the treatment of illness from the knowledge of a cause and effect: up till now the best doctor is the one who reasons the least and observes the most' (Maupertuis, 1965, volume 2, p.417).[11] Finally, as an empiricist, Maupertuis was a Newtonian rather than a Cartesian or Leibnizian. He was the first physicist of significance on the Continent to master Newtonian physics.

However, in metaphysical terms Maupertuis was a rationalist. He was not content to see the world as a chaos of accidents. He was not content with *ad hoc* physical laws. He sought rationalization for physical laws, and for the variety of human action. Despite his mockery of Leibniz's 'principle of sufficient reason' as a truism, and in spite of his willingness to accept gravitation as a brute fact, Maupertuis had not abandoned the rationalist wish for a deeper rationalization of physical laws. His greatest contribution to physics was one such rationalization: the remarkable hypothesis that physical laws obeyed an extremum principle, known as the Principle of Least Action. He first advanced the Principle in the *Accord de Différentes Lois de la Nature* of 1744. (Maupertuis, 1965, volume 4. See Dugas, 1955, pp. 254-75, and Mach, 1960, pp.456-60, for summary and appraisal. See also Samuelson, 1972.)

The background to the Principle of Least Action is the investigation of the laws of the reflection and refraction of light. Certain descriptive laws of reflection and refraction had been established in the 17th century. A simple one, regarding reflection, said that the angle of reflection equals the angle of incidence. It had been noticed that this law implies that any ray of light, originating at point A and ending at point B, after reflecting off surface C, is the shortest path of the many paths which connect point A and point B by two straight lines joined at surface C. Light seemed to get wherever it was going by the shortest route. Could light be distance-minimizing? Such a hypothesis, however, does not fit the case of the refraction of light, where, for example, light passes from air into water. Where light is bent, it does not take the shortest route. Another hypothesis suggests itself. If the speed of light varies from water to air, perhaps refraction could be interpreted as light taking the time-minimizing path; just as time-minimizing travellers do not take the straightest path on the map, but will bend their route to save time. This hypothesis was advanced by Fermat in 1662. It was one of the first minimum hypotheses in physics and was bitterly resisted by the Cartesians.

Pondering this controversy Maupertuis asked himself, 'what preference can there be in this matter for time or distance?'. He concluded that light 'chooses a path which has a very real advantage- *the path which it takes is that by which the quantity of action is the least*' (quoted in Dugas, 1955, p.262). 'Action' was defined as distance multiplied by speed. The principle stated more generally, if vaguely, is that nature minimizes 'her expense in the production of her effects' (Maupertuis, 1965, volume 4, p.22). Maupertuis successfully applied the principle to the reflection and refraction of light, the collision of bodies and the properties of the lever, sometimes defining 'action' in different ways. He concluded that his Principle of Least Action had unified the various laws of physics: it had shown how these laws, which until then had seemed disjointed, were in harmony.

The principle has strong Leibnizian overtones. In fact (apparently unknown to Maupertuis) Leibniz had explored his own maximum principle, in which rays of light followed the path of the 'least difficulty'. Maupertuis was accused of plagiarizing Leibniz. But the truth about priority is not important, since obviously Maupertuis's hypothesis is drenched in Leibnizianism.

The Principle of Least Action has since then done some good work in science. It was developed by Hamilton and Lagrange, it survived Einstein's relativity revolution, and appears in quantum mechanics and the biological principle of homeostasis (Glass, 1970 p.187). But the *lumières* of the 18th century were sceptical: the learned world had grown wary of teleological purposes in nature, and looked doubtfully on any notion of the 'preferences' of light between time and distance. Voltaire rubbished the Principle of Least Action: our arms, he claimed, exert a force of 50lbs to lift 1lb; carps issue millions of eggs to make two fish, oaks issue innumerable acorns to seed one tree: 'there is more profusion than economy in nature' (Voltaire, 1877, volume 38, pp.35-6).

The idea of applying maximum principles to the human world would seem a much more reasonable programme. In fact Maupertuis did approach the notion of maximization in the human world, sometimes faintly, sometimes more strongly. He explicitly saw a role for utility maximization in the formulation of social policy. In his *Éloge de M. de Montesquieu* in 1755 he writes 'The problem which must therefore be resolved by the legislator is this: *the body of men being assembled, the greatest possible sum of happiness must be obtained for it*' (Maupertuis, 1965, volume 3, p.407).[12]

Maupertuis also saw a role for rational maximizing conduct in individual affairs. In his *Essai de Philosophie Morale* of 1749 he mentions the basic idea of trade-offs in maximization:

> Although one can hardly make this comparison with accuracy, there is an infinity of cases where one finds it advantageous to suffer a bad in order to enjoy a good, or to abstain from a good in order to avoid a bad. If the goods and the bads are seen from different distances the comparison becomes even more difficult. It is in all these comparisons that *prudence* consists. (Maupertuis, 1965, volume 1, p.200)

Maupertuis comments, 'It is because it is so difficult to do them [i.e. these comparisons] well that there are so few prudent people ...'. But he adds, 'the infinite variety of the conduct of men results from the different manner in which these calculations are made' (Maupertuis, 1965, volume 1, p.200). So to Maupertuis the variety in human conduct arises merely from the existence of different strategies to secure the same goal of utility maximization. The goal of utility maximisation is now a principle which unifies the explanation of all human behaviour: 'the negro and the philosopher have only the same object: to make their condition better' (Maupertuis, 1965, volume 1, p.226). Strange and self-destructive behaviours: a Guinea slave throwing himself into the sea, the Hindu widow throwing herself on to the pyre; it is all utility maximization. Contrast this unification of human behaviour with Dubos! Contrast it, specifically, with Dubos's explanation of the suicidal tendencies of different nations in terms of different climates. The unificatory purpose of the utility-maximization hypothesis can be compared to the unificatory purpose of the Principle of Least Action. Just as action minimization was meant to show all the different physical laws were in harmony, utility maximization was going to show that all human behaviours were in harmony.[13]

Maupertuis made a few further steps towards the theory of optimization in the context of an individual. He imagined how one might try to calculate whether life was worth living or not by comparing the magnitude of life's ills with the magnitude of life's benefits (Maupertuis, 1965, volume 1, p.201). But it is apparent that Maupertuis could have pursued utility maximization much further. Glass points out that in the *Essai* Maupertuis states that pain is the product of intensity and duration. This means, according to Glass, that to minimize pain would be 'strictly analogous' to minimising 'action': the product of speed and distance (Glass, 1970, p.189). The Law of Minimum Pain as a principle of human action seems to be waiting to be elaborated. Maupertuis even had the elements which could have been the germ of equimarginal conditions: in the *Essai* he posits a dynamized version of diminishing marginal utility, and increasing marginal disutility:

> when one experiences the greatest pleasures that external objects can supply us, one will see that, either the sensation that they excite is of a nature likely to cease promptly, or, that if they last, they soon weaken, becoming insipid and even uncomfortable, if lasting for too long. On the contrary, the pain that external objects cause can last as long as a lifetime; and the longer it lasts the more it becomes unbearable. (Maupertuis, 1965, volume 1, p.209)

In the light of the Law of Least Action and his remarks on utility maximization one can sympathize with the statement by G. Boas in the introduction to a work by Maupertuis on biological inheritance: 'One has the feeling, when reading his works, that he was always on the edge of an important discovery, but never went beyond that edge' (Maupertuis, 1966, p.xxi). One has the feeling he was on the edge of something important in economics as well.

The possibility that Maupertuis was on the edge of a major advance in economics is made all the more intriguing by the fact that he was an early advocate of the importance of economics. In 1755, before the Physiocratic vogue, he wrote of economics, 'This science, neglected, or rather entirely ignored, by the ancient world, is one which demands the most penetration and the most accuracy, and is without contradiction one of the most useful: its problems more difficult than the most difficult problems of Geometry or Algebra, have as an object the wealth of nations, their power and happiness' (Maupertuis, 1965, volume 4, p.416). Maupertuis also speaks admiringly of Melon, who, he says, 'died in my arms'. Maupertuis puts Melon's *Essai Politique sur le Commerce* in the same rank as *L'Esprit des Lois*. Further,

Maupertuis did make one brief foray into economics of his own, in an unpublished 'Lettre sur l'or et l'argent', which has been described by Beeson (1992, pp. 238-40). This paper addresses the problems of a bimetallic standard. It proceeds by an abstract method to analyse the flows of gold and silver between three countries each with their own bimetallic parities. Beeson speculates that there may have been other papers on economics; his unpublished papers were burnt, on his instructions, following his death.

It remains the case that the explorations of rational maximization by Maupertuis and Bernoulli had little direct influence on 18th century economics. Halévy asserts, without substantiation, that Bentham borrowed some of his formula for the 'moral calculus' from Maupertuis (Halévy, 1928, p.19).[14] Daniel Bernoulli's analysis of the St Petersburg Paradox found its way into discussions of probability; D'Alembert comments unfavourably on it in the *Encylopédie* (Maistrov, 1974, p.124). Stark points out that Bentham justifies the irrationality of accepting fair bets by reference to declining marginal utility (Bentham, 1843, volume 1, p.306; volume 3, p.230), and infers that it is 'probable' that Bentham had read Bernoulli's 1738 paper. But the Leibnizian investigation of the 'science of happiness' seems to have left no mark beyond these meagre specks. The seeds of neoclassical optimization failed to sprout. The Lockean vision of man as short sighted, wilful and self-destructive seemed more persuasive.

3.5 Conclusion

In the fragmentary economic writings of Dubos and Bernoulli we see relatively pure expressions of the two alternatives offered by Locke and Leibniz to economic inquiry, one rationalist and the other anti-rationalist.

The anti-rationalist approach of Dubos sought to remove intellect from the growth of knowledge, from human activity and human judgements. Combined with his subjectivism, which encouraged the notion that everything was relative, no general or theoretical economics was possible in his approach. But the possibility of 'historical' or 'cultural' economics remained.

The rationalist Bernoulli, following Leibniz's lead, initiated the investigation of the science of happiness, and provided a theory of the rational utility maximizer in situations of uncertainty. This was generalized by Maupertuis into a vision in which all human conduct was unified by the goal of utility maximization. The possibility of what we might call 'proto neoclassical' economics was here.

However in the third quarter of the 18th century, these pure expressions of rationalism and anti-rationalism found little development. The highly empirical, specific methods of Dubos and the political arithmeticians were not imitated; neither was the mathematical theory of utility maximization of Daniel Bernoulli. Economic doctrine instead attempted mixed treatments of the questions which divided rationalism and anti-rationalism.

Notes

1   Bonno identified Dubos's letters as the informational source for the anonymous *An Introductory Discourse to Churchill's Collection of Voyages,* which has sometimes been attributed to John Locke (Locke, 1823, volume 10).

2   Kaiser (1989) states Dubos's principal debt in this theory is owed to Hugo Grotius.

3   Charles Davenant (1654-1714) was a sometime Tory MP of French sympathies, who had been cultivated by French political agents in London (Waddell, 1958-59).

4   The closest thing to an 'inductive law' in political arithmetic appears in Davenant's *Essay upon the Probable Methods of Making a People Gainers in the Balance of Trade* of 1699. This includes a quantitative relation between 'the defect in harvest' and the consequent rise in price; the so called 'King-Davenant Law'.

5   After study at the Paris School of Anatomy, Petty was appointed Professor of Anatomy at Oxford in 1651, and in 1652 physician-general to the army in Ireland. He was removed from this post in 1659 at the age of 36, the last time he practised medicine as his principal occupation.

6   Petty saw a parallel between the 'foundation of medicine' (i.e. anatomy) and political arithmetic. Petty called his first exercise in political arithmetic the *Political Anatomy of Ireland.* His preface consists of analogy between a medical dissection and what he performs in the subsequent pages: he sees himself as identifying, for example, the liver, spleen and lungs of Ireland.

7   In London Dubos had attended the hanging of a forger.

8   One illustration of this interest is Mandeville's *Enquiry into the Origin of Honour, and the Usefulness of Christianity in War* of 1732.

9   The promise of the title of the incomplete fourth part of Bernoulli's book, 'Application of the Previous Study to Civil, Moral and Economic Problems' was not fulfilled. The unfinished part contains 'only' the Law of Large Numbers (Maistrov, 1974, p.67).

10   This paper was published in 1738. Bassett (1987) states it was presented in 1731.

11   Maupertuis praises Sydenham as the modern Hippocrates.

12   This may be compared with Hutcheson's maxim of 1725, 'That action is best, which procures the greatest happiness for the greatest numbers'. The 'greatest happiness for the greatest numbers' is ambiguous to the point of meaninglessness.

---

13 In this connection it is worth recalling that one motive for Leibniz's development of calculus was to unify the treatment of mathematical problems.

14 Smith had a copy of Maupertuis's complete works in his personal library, but the only direct trace of Maupertuis in Smith is a note on the figure of the earth in Smith's *History of Astronomy* (Smith, 1982a, p.101).

4. The empirical optimists: Hutcheson and Mandeville

This chapter turns from the study of contrast to a study of parallels; from a study of divergence to that of convergence. It analyses how two authors, Mandeville and Hutcheson, combined rationalist and anti-rationalist elements in composing a picture of the human world. These two authors would be surprised to see themselves grouped together. Hutcheson, especially, saw his ethics as highly antagonistic to Mandeville's 'licentious System'.[1] But it is reason and order which are the subject of this study, not vice and virtue. The critical point for our purpose is that both these authors absorbed rationalist themes in metaphysics and anti-rationalist themes in epistemology and psychology. They both saw the world as a functioning order and human nature as essentially uniform. At the same time they both maintained that experience is the source of knowledge, and that human nature is guided by passion, not reason.

4.1 Francis Hutcheson and the 'face of Moral Goodness'

Francis Hutcheson (1694-1746) held the Chair of Moral Philosophy at the University of Glasgow from 1730 until 1746. Among his students was Adam Smith, who later 'always spoke in the terms of warmest admiration' of Hutcheson's lectures (Smith, 1982a, p.271). Smith's works come closer in flavour to Hutcheson than any other major writer.

Hutcheson was a student of the human soul, and his various disquisitions from 1725 to 1742 ran over many departments, including aesthetics, morals, jurisprudence and political economy. His sources, like his interests, were diverse: his biographer comments 'he borrows alike from Descartes, Locke, Wolff and Berkeley, so that the final result is an eclectic treatment ...' (Scott, 1966, p.261).[2] Hutcheson created from these and others a compound of rationalist and anti-rationalist sentiments.

In matters of metaphysics, Hutcheson was a rationalist. He saw the world as a harmonious structure. 'Observe all nature as far as our knowledge extends; we find the contrivance good. The alleged blemishes are now known to be either the unavoidable attendants or consequences of a structure and of laws subservient to advantages which quite over-ballance these inconveniences...' (Hutcheson, 1969, volume 1, p.180). Such views had earlier received a strong expression in Leibniz's *Théodicée*, published in 1710. A comparable stimulus was provided in 1711 by the *Inquiry Concerning Virtue and Merit* by Anthony Ashley Cooper, the third Earl of Shaftesbury (1671-1713).[3]

In keeping with his rationalist metaphysics, Hutcheson saw uniformity as 'copiously diffused throughout the universe'. To rebut the notion of the world as fickle and extraordinary he writes mockingly of readers (such as Locke) with a taste for travel writing, and the 'wondrous *Credulity* of some Gentleman of great Pretensions in other Matters to caution of Assent, for these *marvellous Memoirs* of Monks, Friars, Sea-Captains, Pirates' (Hutcheson, 1971, p.204). The memoirs of monks, friars, sea-captains and pirates: exactly the books which Dubos and Locke had exchanged letters upon. Hutcheson's stress on the uniform character of the human world is clearly a massive deviation from Locke.[4]

Rationalist in metaphysics, Hutcheson remained an empiricist in epistemology. It is empirical science which has shown how the contrivance of the world is good. It is 'Our present discoveries in natural Philosophy' which have refuted the ancient atheist's belief as to the incoherence of nature. Similarly, Hutcheson's favoured grounds for the proof of a God were empirical, not the 'existential' ones which Locke favours in the *Essay* (Locke, 1959, IV, x).[5]

Hutcheson was also anti-rationalist in psychology. It was his opinion that we rely on our appetites, rather than reason, to guide our conduct. 'The weakness of our reason, and the avocations rising from the infirmities and necessities of our nature, are so great that very few men could ever have formed those long deductions of reason which show some actions to be in the whole advantageous to the agent, and their contraries pernicious' (Hutcheson, 1973, p.25).

Hutcheson extended the notion that we are rightly guided by our appetites, rather than our reason, to aesthetics. Aesthetics in the early 18th century was dominated by the Cartesian doctrine that reason was the proper tool for the detection, analysis and appreciation of beauty. These claims had already been abruptly challenged by Dubos, who had made a 'sixth sense' of beauty. To Hutcheson, too, our judgement of beauty is a sense, comparable to the sense of sight. The object which excited our sense of beauty was 'uniformity amidst variety' (Hutcheson, 1973, p.47).[6] Hutcheson believed that the power of 'uniformity amidst variety' to excite our sense of beauty was so strong, that it sometimes enticed philosophers into adopting overly simple systems based on a few general principles.

> It is no less easy to see into what absurd attempts men have been led by this sense of beauty, and an affectation of obtaining it in other sciences as well as the mathematics. 'Twas this probably which set Descartes on that hopeful project of deducing all human knowledge from one proposition, viz. *Cogito ergo sum*; ... Mr. Leibniz has an equal affection for his favourite principle of a *sufficient reason* .... This observation is a strong proof that men perceive the beauty of uniformity in the sciences, since they are led into unnatural deductions by pursuing it too far. (Hutcheson, 1973, pp.51,52)

Smith later expressed a similar caution against this partiality towards the beauty of system (1982b, p. 299).

Hutcheson extended the sphere of the senses to include moral judgements; they too were based, not on reason, but on sense, a *moral sense*. (What are moral judgements, but a judgement of the beauty of actions?) In the best uniformitarian manner he took this moral sense to be universal. And he took it to be far more basic to human nature than reason. Hutcheson had far more trust in the moral sense of humankind than in its reasoning powers: 'And it is strange, that *Reason* is universally allow'd to Men, not withstanding all the stupid ridiculous Opinions receiv'd in many Places ... the absurd Practises which prevail in the World, are much better Arguments that men have no *Reason*, than that they have no *moral Sense* of *Beauty* in Actions' (Hutcheson, 1969, volume 1, p.208). Hutcheson's separation of moral judgements from reason was accepted by Smith and Hume. It also pushed back the borders of the proper domain of reason on another front.

In summary, Hutcheson's principal contribution was to give an anti-rationalist basis to the notion of the world as a beneficent system. The proof of the beneficent order was made firmly empirical, not philosophical. The mechanism of its beneficent operation was made to depend, not on the rationality of men, but on their psychological constitution (their 'moral sense') which predisposed them to virtuous actions. This moral sense operated universally, and made a mockery of the travellers' tales of 'wild nations' which suggested otherwise.

A defect of Hutcheson's vision of a beneficent order is its reliance on the existence of a 'moral sense'. This rather hopeful supposition is not very compelling. A sharper advocacy of the existence of a beneficent world order required a harder judgement of human nature. This advocacy would be especially helped by an argument to the effect that even an immoral human nature was not inconsistent with the operation of a beneficent order. This argument was supplied by Bernard Mandeville.

4.2 Bernard Mandeville and the 'despicable Foundation'

Bernard Mandeville (1670-1733) was born in a time and place which served him well to observe the clash of ideas. His medical studies at the University of Leiden were undertaken in the shadow of the 'hatred' (his word) between the Aristotelians and Cartesians. His doctoral dissertation was a Cartesian exercise, in which he denied that animals had the power of thought. But as a student Mandeville must also have been exposed to the highly anti-rationalist philosophy of Pierre Bayle.

Bayle (1647-1706) had won celebrity while teaching at the *École Illustre* in Rotterdam, at the same time as Mandeville attended the Erasmian School there. (Mandeville may have attended Bayle's lectures.)[7] Bayle was an extreme sceptic of all aspirations to belief which was both true and reasonable. He advanced his sceptical views in his *Dictionnaire Historique et Critique*. This 'Dictionary' was originally designed as a compilation of the errors of earlier historians; so instead of being a testimony to knowledge, as an encyclopedia is usually conceived, it was to be a testimony to the difficulty of knowledge. Its huge incoherent mass of detail seemed to deny any hope that human knowledge may be planned or ordered. In its footnotes, which account for most of the text, the pretence to true and reasonable belief was laid waste. Reason 'can only discover to man his ignorance and weakness' (Bayle, 1734, 'Manichees', Note D); it is 'ever impotent' and only increases 'mischief' (Bayle, 1734, 'Ovid', Note H). Mandeville must have read the Dictionary closely; critics have identified 70 entries in it which Mandeville made use of in his *Free Thoughts on Religion, the Church and National Happiness* of 1720 (James, 1975).[8]

In 1691 Mandeville obtained a medical degree, and began to develop a specialism in 'hysteria'. In 1699 he moved to England and shortly began devising what was to become the masterpiece of his eccentric genius, the *Fable of the Bees*.

The predominant theme of the *Bees* is that human beings have a *nature*, but that human nature is distinguished from animal nature only by certain human vices: pride, envy and deceit. Our nature is not distinguished from that of animals by our rationality. Man, to Mandeville, is not by *nature* a rational creature. Reason is only a product of the environment. 'Thinking, and Reasoning justly, as Mr *Lock* has rightly observed, require Time and Practice ... Man is a rational Creature, but he is not endued with Reason when he comes into the World; nor can he afterwards put it on when he pleases, at once, as he may a Garment' (Mandeville, 1924, volume 2, p.190).[9] For that reason, '... there is nothing, in which Men differ so immensely from one another, as they do in the Exercise of this Faculty [i.e. thinking]: the difference between them in Height, Bulk, Strength, are trifling, in Comparison' (Mandeville, 1924, volume 2, p.170). The similarity to Locke, and the contrast with Leibniz, on this point is plain.

Our reason, says Mandeville, has no responsibility for the social features of human society. He appositely observes that the very structure of human society, that is, parenthood and children, does not emerge through design. Our reason also has little responsibility for the arts and technologies of human society. Their development is instead owed to humankind's use of ordinary experience: '... it is incredible, how many useful Cautions, Shifts and Stratagems, they will learn to practise by Experience and Imitation ...' (Mandeville, 1924, volume 2, p.139). Mandeville claims that many useful inventions and techniques are the result of the experience of the unlettered. His specific example is the principles of the navigation of sailing craft, the results of which can be demonstrated theoretically, but which were in reality learnt by 'tedious experience'. To Mandeville 'learned reasoning' is rarely the source of technical improvement: 'They are very seldom the same Sort of People, those that invent Arts, and Improvements in them, and commonly practis'd by such, as are idle and indolent, that are fond of Retirement, hate Business, and take delight in Speculation: whereas none succeed oftener in the first, than active, stirring and laborious Men' (Mandeville, 1924, volume 2, p.144). This attribution of the useful arts to the experience of everyday life, rather than refined learning, has plain parallels in Dubos and Locke.

Mandeville's stress on experience and disdain for 'speculation' was manifested in his medical principles (as was the case with Locke). Mandeville elaborated his medical views at considerable length in his *Treatise on Hypochondriack and Hysteric Diseases* of 1730 (Mandeville, 1976).[10] A large part of the *Treatise* is occupied by a discussion of methodological issues in medicine. Mandeville is revealed there to be a vehement 'empirick'. Like Locke, he praised the 'great Sydenham' (Mandeville, 1976, p.118).[11] Like Sydenham he espoused a fundamental empiricist epistemological principle: that the surface is observable and therefore knowable, but the deep, underlying causes are not knowable. 'Physicians, with the rest of Mankind, are wholly ignorant of the first Principles and constituent Parts of Things, ... and consequently all the Medicines they make use of. There is no Art that has less Certainty than theirs, and the most valuable Knowledge in it arises from Observation ...' (Mandeville, 1924, volume 2, p.161). Therefore, to Mandeville, as with Sydenham and Locke, fundamental medical researches in anatomy, botany and chemistry served no purpose except to gratify a doctor's pride.

Since accurate medical explanation is always uncertain, Mandeville maintained that physicians make themselves useful only by concentrating on prediction. The infallible test of the worth of any doctor is clear and true predictions (Mandeville, 1976, p.71) and he urged doctors to make 'bold' predictions.

Mandeville allowed that speculative systems sometimes appear to assist predictions, as in astronomy (Mandeville, 1976, pp. 120-124). He observed that there are several theories of the solar system 'exactly delineated after a Geometrical Manner' which foretell astronomical events with accuracy. He drew three conclusions from this. First, astronomy is an indication of how much observation can instruct, not in a period of 25 years, the brief span of a single doctor's career, but over a period of 2,000 years. The suggestion is that if medical observation is practised for as long a period as astronomical observation is practised for as long a period as astronomical observation has been, medicine could advance to the same degree as astronomy. Mandeville's second conclusion is that hypotheses are just 'rules' which make 'a shew'. In modern parlance Mandeville was an instrumentalist. Mandeville's third conclusion is that predictive success is a poor proof of the theory:

> ... we may learn how weak and fallacious a Proof, the Solution of the Symptoms from an Hypothesis must be, of our being acquainted with the true Cause of the Distemper; when from this Instance of Astronomy it is evident, that the same *Phenomena* exactly answer to different Hypotheses, of which at best only one can be true. (Mandeville, 1976, p.122)

Not only may contrary theories both give correct predictions, Mandeville also believed that typically theories are vague enough to conform with any observed situation: 'A Witty Man that can express himself in good Language, and is tolerably vers'd in the Theory of Physick, may, by the help of a well-contriv'd *Hypothesis*, find out probable Causes, floridly account for every Symptom ...' (Mandeville, 1976, p.69). By explaining everything, they explain nothing. In summary, Mandeville believed that principles and hypothesis are a poor resource for prediction.

The contrast between Mandeville's treatment of astronomical hypothesis and Smith's treatment in his *History of Astronomy* indicates the bite of Mandeville's anti-rationalism. To Smith the psychological function of scientific hypothesis is to give ease to mental operations; to Mandeville its purpose is to gratify pride. To Smith there are logical considerations governing the succession of astronomical hypotheses. To Mandeville there are not: the succession of hypotheses is governed not by logical considerations, but by a 'perfect state of war' between the rivals. The disputations and verbal exchanges which figure so prominently in these wars have little to do with the advance knowledge. Language, according to Mandeville, is in origin an instrument of cajolery, not communication.[12] And even if used as an instrument of communication, language is a feeble device for that purpose, since it can communicate only a meagre part of our experience: 'What a Variety of different Hues there is in the several Mixtures, that all come under the denomination of Cloth-colour, and have no other name ...' (Mandeville, 1976, p.61). In spite of this poverty of words, Mandeville noted regretfully that his 'talkative' age sprouted hypothesis in a competition for distinction by the best talkers (Mandeville, 1976, p.127).

To summarize, epistemologically and psychologically Mandeville is not far from Locke; there is the same belittling of reason, the same stress on ordinary experience, the same dissatisfaction with words. But metaphysically he is very different.

Mandeville was uniformitarian. He is distinguished from Locke by an incuriosity about the variety of human forms. His taste avoided refinement; but it also avoided the outlandish or bizarre; his works contain no tales of 'Monks, Friars, Sea-Captains and Pirates'. His taste was stolid, earthy and plain. This left him with an ahistorical, abstract method. 'When I have a Mind to dive into the Origin of any Maxim or political Invention, for the Use of Society in general, I don't trouble my Head with inquiring after the Time or Country, in which it was first heard of, nor what others have wrote or said about it; but I go directly to the Fountain Head, human Nature itself ...' (Mandeville, 1924, volume 2, p.128). Mandeville in this passage is advocating the use of a universal human nature as a tool of analysis.

Mandeville was also distinguished from Locke by his conception of society as a sort of system. There is a kind of self-regulating, interlocking, self-supporting, well-adjustedness in the parts of society. Even those parts which commonsense suggests damage the system actually help it work. Mandeville, notoriously, finds a usefulness in 'Vice'. Pride and luxury, for example, are economically useful: they give life to industry. So vice is not a dysfunction; it is not even a proof of dysfunction. In a similar way Mandeville even finds a useful purpose in great calamities. The Fire of London, for example, supplies work to tradesmen.

Further, Mandeville's perception of a useful order went beyond the economic system of human society. In the neglected 5th dialogue between Cleomenes and Horatio in the *Bees*, Mandeville painted a picture of an entire universe designed by a wise Creator in which all parts interlock, and in which the most jarring elements secretly serve a useful end. Wars are useful because they prevent the world from overpopulating. These wars take an especially heavy toll on men. But as a compensation, women die from 'calamities of their own sex', to keep males and females balanced. Men also face an additional heavy toll from work hazards, but for this 'nature has made a provision' by ensuring that more boys than girls are born. But not too many more boys, since a scarcity of women relative to men would cause discord, as well as deprive the world of that useful phenomenon, the impoverished woman, who sends her impoverished children out to perform 'hard and dirty' labour, upon which 'all Comforts of Life, in the civilis'd State, have their unavoidable dependence' (Mandeville, 1924, volume 2, p.259).

Could not nature have made human beings affectionate and solved the resulting population problem by rendering them largely infertile? Mandeville considered this inconsistent with the supreme foresight of the Creator. 'But to make a Scheme first, and afterwards to mend it, when it proves defective, is the Business of finite Wisdom ... Infinite Wisdom is not liable to Errors or Mistakes ...' (Mandeville, 1924, volume 2, p.256).[13] In any case, if men had been meek and infertile 'there could not have been that Stir and Variety, nor, upon the whole, that Beauty in the World ...' (Mandeville, 1924, volume 2, p.260).

Further, Mandeville contends that when contemplating the scheme of things we should not consider only the advantage of the human species: '... it is highly probable, that there are thousands of things, and perhaps our own Machines among them, that in the vast System of the Universe are now serving some very wise Ends, which we shall never know' (Mandeville, 1924, volume 2, p.244). He revives the Principle of Sufficient Reason to show that 'it is ridiculous to think, that the Universe was made for our sake' (Mandeville, 1924, volume 2, p.261). The sun is so large it must serve some other purpose than merely lighting our earth since a smaller sun, closer to us would have been sufficient for that purpose. The comfort of humanity is not a 'sufficient reason' for the size and position for the sun, and therefore the sun must have some other function.

This notion of a grand function directing all the parts of the universe, which makes sense of all its apparent cruelties and madnesses, is hardly reminiscent of Locke. It is reminiscent of Leibniz. There is something of Dr Pangloss in Mandeville: whatever he thinks upon, child labour, war, fire, it is all for the best; there is a huge well-designed system of which we are one tiny uncomprehending part.

So Mandeville was not the supreme anti-rationalist, as Kaye tried to paint him. In the 5th dialogue Mandeville embraced the supreme rationalist Leibniz, or at least his conception of God designing a universe 'incomprehensible beyond human reach' and placing man there as part of the system.[14] He was also rationalist in seeking uniformity in foundations, in this case in human nature. So Mandeville supported the metaphysical aspect of Leibniz while retaining and advocating the epistemology and psychology of Locke. In all this Mandeville is not at war with Hutcheson, but quite at one with him. (Similarly Mandeville's relations to Shaftesbury are far less antithetical than his own remarks suggest. See Primer, 1975.)

Mandeville's strongly rationalist vision was important in the development of classical economics. To be sure, Classical economics did not take up Mandeville's extreme rationalistic optimism, which found good fortune even in calamity. But the notion that 'a most beautiful Superstructure may be rais'd upon a rotten and despicable Foundation' (Mandeville, 1924, volume 2, p.64) was influential. Mandeville had shown that vice was not dysfunctional, or symptomatic of dysfunction. 'Vice', especially egotism, could be manipulated by the right incentives to further the public interest. This doctrine did not by itself imply a *laissez-faire* stance; it is well known that Mandeville adopted many particular positions which were contrary to *laissez-faire* (Viner, 1953; Landreth, 1975). To Mandeville the 'dexterous politician' was still needed to harness the power of 'vice' to drive the public good. Mandeville was not mindful of the notion that competitive exchange could harness that power. But the maxim of 'Private Vices, Public Benefits' is nevertheless highly conducive to that notion. Mandeville made more plausible the existence of a beneficent order existing amidst the tumult of the market.

4.3 Conclusion

Hutcheson and Mandeville provided a hybrid of rationalist and anti-rationalist sentiments. They absorbed the uniformitarianism of rationalism; and they absorbed its vision of a harmoniously operating world order. But they also absorbed the empiricism of anti-rationalism, and the assumption that humanity was guided by passions (not reason) in its conduct. They argued for the existence of a harmonious order on empirical grounds, and claimed that it worked by way of human passions, even ugly ones. This hybrid of metaphysical rationalism and epistemological and psychological anti-rationalism was extremely influential on the social thought of the 18th century. This hybrid was, however, a matter of 'pre-analytic vision' rather than science. To implement it scientifically required an epistemological shift away from the simple empiricism they employed.

Notes

1 Kaye grants similarities between Hutcheson and Mandeville, but dismisses these similarities as 'superficial' (Mandeville, 1924, volume 2, p.345).

2 Hutcheson describes his *System of Moral Philosophy* as a 'compound' of Cicero, Aristotle, Pufendorf and 'that worthy and ingenious man the late Professor Gershom Carmichael of Glasgow' (quoted in Taylor, 1965, p.25).

3 Shaftesbury's *Inquiry* sent Leibniz into raptures. 'The turn of the discourse, its style, the dialogue, the new Platonism, the method of arguing through questions, but above all, the grandeur and beauty of the ideas, their luminous enthusiasm, the apostrophe to deity, ravished me and brought me to a state of ecstasy' (Leibniz, 1969, p.633).

4 Hutcheson in this regard also resembles Shaftesbury, who had faulted 'the credulous Mr Locke with his Indian, barbarian stories of wild nations ...'Twas Mr Locke that struck at all fundamentals, threw all order and virtue out of the world ...' (Shaftesbury, 1900, p.403).

5 Locke occasionally makes fleeting reference to the 'harmonious design' of the universe (1954, p.153), but there is little in his works to persuade the reader of it.

6 Hutcheson's position has a similarity with Leibniz's doctrine that '... unity in plurality is nothing but harmony, and ... there flows from this harmony the order from which beauty arises ...' (Leibniz, 1969, p.426). Hutcheson differs from Leibniz in that he does not attempt to reduce the sensation of beauty to a 'confused' idea of harmony.

7 Popkin says Mandeville was 'apparently' a student of Bayle at Rotterdam (Popkin, 1967, p.259). James (1975) states it is not known if they met.

8 In the *Bees* Mandeville imitated Bayle's technique of huge footnotes.

9 See also Mandeville's rebuttal of Shaftesbury's optimism about reason (Mandeville, 1924, volume 1, p.324).

10 See Rousseau (1975) for a discussion of Mandeville's medical views.

11 Sydenham had a great interest in hysteria. He believed it accounted for a very large proportion of all illnesses (Schneck, 1957).

12 '... the first Design of Speech was to persuade others, either to give Credit to what the speaking Person would have them believe; or else to act or suffer such Things, as he would compel them to act or suffer, if they were entirely in his Power' (Mandeville, 1924, volume 2, p.289).

13 This is reminiscent of Leibniz's arguments against Newton's gravitational theory of the orbits of the planets: that theory necessitated, Leibniz held, the episodic intervention of God in order to keep the system operating, and was therefore inconsistent with the infinite foresight of the Creator.

14 This dialogue obviously embarrasses Kaye's thesis that Mandeville was a thoroughgoing anti-rationalist (see Kaye in Mandeville, 1924, volume 2, p.21). Kaye therefore supposes that Cleomenes is not always the voice of Mandeville, despite

Mandeville's claim that 'Cleomenes is my friend, and speaks my sentiments ...' (Mandeville, 1924, volume 2, p.21). Kaye contends that in the 5th dialogue Horatio is the voice of Mandeville and Cleomenes is the voice of 'religious orthodoxy'. This allows Horatio to rebut orthodoxy without Mandeville's orthodoxy being impugned. But does Horatio rebut Cleomenes?

5. Hume and the restoration of the *a priori*

In the last chapter it was argued that Hutcheson and Mandeville made common cause with anti-rationalists in removing knowledge, morality and beauty from the rule of reason. At the same time they sided with the rationalists in assuming human nature was uniform, and that there existed a functioning world order. Their 'empirical optimism', their notion of a functioning world order proved by plain fact, became very popular in the 18th century.[1]

However, their combination of empiricism and uniformitarianism was much less compelling; it is difficult for an empiricist to assert the uniformity of the human world in the face of the bounty of reports of its apparent variety. One may say that the combination of empiricism and uniformitarianism as attempted by Hutcheson and Mandeville was too frail to survive; it would either be broken or strengthened. Montesquieu (1689-1755) broke it: he took the obvious lesson of empiricism and rejected the uniformitarianism. David Hume (1711-76), by contrast, sought to strengthen the combination. He tried to fasten uniformitarianism to empiricism by suggesting how the two may be made consistent.

Ironically, the adherence of Montesquieu and Hume to empiricism encouraged in both the utilization of more 'theoretical' methods. By accepting the empiricist lesson that human societies were heterogeneous, Montesquieu damaged one of the principal tools of empiricism: induction from past and foreign experience. By reconciling uniformitarianism with empiricism, Hume provided 'theorists' with general principles to work with: namely, certain empirically confirmed uniformities. So Hume restored the method of principles in the eyes of the empiricists by establishing the empirical credentials of general principles. He simultaneously rescued empiricism from the fact-grubbing political arithmeticians on one hand, and general principles from 'profound philosophers' on the other, and gave the two combined to the emerging social sciences. He set the stage epistemologically for Smith's analytic implementation of

62

the vision of Hutcheson and Mandeville, and Smith's more thoroughgoing reconciliation of the *a posteriori* and *a priori*.

There was one other dimension to the synthesis of Hutcheson and Mandeville which Hume reinforced. They had coupled their metaphysical rationalism with psychological anti-rationalism. They had retained their optimistic vision of a functioning world order in spite of their belief that humankind was naturally passionate, rather than naturally reasonable. Human reason seemed unnecessary for a functioning human order. Hume went still further. He denied reason could ever be the foundation of a human order, and suggested that optimism is possible because of our lack of reason, rather than in spite of it.

This chapter begins by outlining the responses of Montesquieu and Hume to the tension between empiricism and uniformitarianism. It then turns to Hume's response to the friction between Hutcheson's and Mandeville's optimism about a world order and their pessimism about human reason.

5.1 Montesquieu and the spirit of relativity

Montesquieu's work can be conceived, like that of Hutcheson and Mandeville, as a work of integration of rationalism and anti-rationalism. All three were empirical and subjectivist in tendency. But Montesquieu's anti-rationalism went further. By accepting the apparent lessons of empiricism and subjectivism, Montesquieu rejected the uniformitarianism of Hutcheson and Mandeville. He adopted a relativist position, which emphasized diversity over uniformity. Montesquieu's *L'Esprit des Lois* of 1748, with its stress on 'spirit', mentalities and national character, exemplifies this emphasis. It provided the strongest development of the germ of time-, place- and culture-specific approach of Dubos.

Therefore, Montesquieu's work was to some extent an articulation of Dubos's comprehensive challenge to general principles.[2] Montesquieu's judgement of Dubos as a 'great man' is more than mere courtesy. It is an acknowledgement of Montesquieu's debts to Dubos.[3] Montesquieu's belief in the importance of climate, for example, seems to have been initially stimulated by Dubos (Shackleton, 1961, p.303). Dubos had advanced a climatic explanation of national character in Chapter xv of Section II of the *Réflexions*. In that theory, which is reminiscent of Locke's research into 'miasmas', Dubos explained 'cultural' differences in terms of the effect of the atmosphere on the human body. By this hypothesis Dubos explained the contrast between the relish for intellectual discussion in his own lifetime, with the total indifference to such activity four centuries earlier. Dubos had argued 'elegantly in favour of climatic influence' in Madame de Lambert's salon, of which Montesquieu was a member (Shackleton, 1961, p.34).

Montesquieu's relativism also received encouragement from Dubos's subjectivist theory of beauty. The beautiful, the good, the noble, the great, the perfect are all relative to the observer, said Montesquieu. Rationalists, he wrote, had made a fatal error in denying this. Malebranche, for example, had fallen into 1,000 sophisms owing to the neglect of this principle (Montesquieu, 1949, volume 1, p.1537). One can also see a parallel with Dubos in one of Montesquieu's remarks on the relation between the intellect and senses. In the *Esprit des Lois* Montesquieu describes reason as the 'the noblest, the most perfect, the most exquisite of our senses' (Montesquieu, 1989, p.337). This sensualization of the intellect forms a parallel with Dubos's identification of judgements of beauty with a sixth sense.

Montesquieu's relativism, his emphasis on national character, and his stress on highly variable climatic factors, means that in metaphysical terms Montesquieu was anti-rationalist.[4] He was especially repelled by the rationalist passion for uniformity. In Chapter 18 of the 29th book of *L'Esprit* he struck at this passion with disdain: 'There are certain ideas of uniformity that sometimes seize great spirits, ... but that infallibly strike small ones' (Montesquieu, 1989, p.617). Such passages infuriated later rationalist advocates such as Turgot and Condorcet. Montesquieu's disdain would seem to spell the end of general principles.

However, for all his accommodation of the outlandish and singular, Montesquieu's work also obviously contains a strong rationalist element. It is thereby distanced from Dubos, and can for this reason be regarded as a work of synthesis of rationalism and anti-rationalism. Montesquieu begins *L'Esprit* by denying that the world is a matter of blind chance. Rather, the world is a matter of laws. The laws are not arbitrary, but are adaptations to the mentality and material conditions of the society they govern. So there is a rationale behind the relativity of laws.

Further, Montesquieu suggests that the world is a system. It is not, admittedly, the 'system of hierarchy' favoured by Cartesian rationalists. Rather it is a system of mutual interdependence. The concept of a system of mutual interdependence did not originate with Montesquieu. Expressions of the idea can be found in Shaftesbury, Dubos and Mandeville.[5] Critically, Mandeville had already suggested that the antithetical character of society's composing elements actually constituted the basis of the social order.[6] Such an idea was rich meat to Montesquieu; from diversity arises harmony. Montesquieu made such a notion famous. He analysed the English constitution in terms of the mutual balancing of its parts. He also used it to analyse feudalism.[7] He underlined his conception of mutual interdependence by deploying the words *balance* and *équilibre*.[8]

The notion of a structure of mutual interdependence became popular in the 18th century, and it appears in Galiani, Hume, Condillac, Turgot and Smith. Hume studied the balance of power in international politics, and puzzled over the absence of this notion in the Ancients: how could they be oblivious to such an 'obvious' notion? (Hume, 1987, pp.332-341). Condillac announced that 'Our universe is only a large balance' (Condillac, 1947, volume 1, p.676). Closer to earth, in the 15th chapter of the *Traité des Systèmes* Condillac extended this notion of equilibrium to the social world: society is an 'artificial body' composed of parts, the social classes, each with a 'reciprocal action' on the other.[9] Smith analysed feudalism as a system of mutual interdependence.[10] Smith and Condillac's vision of a system of mutual interdependence between the social classes is clearly antagonistic to the structure of hierarchy frequently associated with conservative or 'radical' theories of social structure. But, more importantly for this study, it is also suggestive of an equilibrium in an economic system consisting of markets and prices acting reciprocally on one another.

But if Montesquieu's belief in a heterogeneous social universe was reconciled to his belief in an ordered social universe by way of the notion of mutual interdependence, it was more difficult to reconcile his vision of a heterogeneous social universe with his empiricism. For although empiricism encourages this vision of a heterogeneous social universe, it is also true that the same vision discourages empiricism, by making induction infeasible. How can one hope to learn from past experience (or foreign experience) if truth is totally time- and place-specific? This is perhaps why Montesquieu, unlike Dubos, did not see wisdom as consisting of the accumulation of experience over long periods of time. Rather he saw wisdom as something provided by lawgivers of genius, such as Solon, whom he admired. So Montesquieu's empiricism actually led back to a highly rationalist attitude to the acquisition of truth: the world is a problem to be solved by those with genius.

5.2 Hume's reconciliation of principles and empirics

Unlike Montesquieu, Hume retained the uniformitarianism of Hutcheson and Mandeville. He buttressed his uniformitarianism by his rebuttal of 'material' theories of human behaviour. Dubos and Montesquieu had relied on highly variable material factors (climate, soil, topography) to explain human conduct. Hume strongly rejected such material determinants of human character. Most of Hume's 1748 essay 'Of National Characters' is devoted to discrediting the explanation of national character in terms of climate. If climate is an important determinant of manners and morals, how can we explain the difference between human behaviour at Wapping and at the Court of St James's? Hume thereby disposed of a doctrine which, if true, would have imposed a heterogeneity on humankind by virtue of the heterogeneity of its climate.

But Hume accepted empiricism, and empiricism posed a substantial threat to uniformitarianism. But (unlike Montesquieu) he did not abandon uniformitarianism in the face of the threat. Instead he eliminated the threat by reconciling uniformitarianism and empiricism.

Hume's reconciliation rests in part on the proposition that reports of strange human behaviour are deceptive. He argued in favour of this assertion in a dialogue at the close of *An Enquiry Concerning the Principles of Morals*, published in 1751. In this dialogue Palamedes returns from Fourli, a country 'whose inhabitants have ways of thinking, in many things, particularly in morals, diametrically opposite to ours' (Hume, 1975, p.324). Palamedes tells of his companion in Fourli, Alcheic, who was 'extremely celebrated' for his virtue. We learn that Alcheic was a pederast who had married his own sister, had murdered his father and had assassinated his 'intimate friend' Usbek, an act for which he received special acclaim.

Once Palamedes has finished his story, Hume alerts the reader that Palamedes's apparently fantastic 'travellers' tale' is composed merely from the chronicles of Greece and Rome. Further, says Hume, one could contrive apparently fantastic travellers' tales from contemporary France and England: duelling over trifles; 'jails, where every art of plaguing and tormenting the unhappy prisoners is carefully studied', even 'the superiority of females'. The suggestion is that what is commonplace in the West could be made to appear strange by the device of a foreigner's travellers' tale of the West. (This suggestion was not new: this was the gimmick of Montesquieu's *Lettres Persanes*.) [11] The lesson, evidently, is that since the commonplace can be made so easily to appear strange, we should be ready to suspect that the reportedly strange is actually familiar. Therefore, said Hume, one need not conclude from travellers' tales that 'fashion, vogue, custom and law' are the chief foundation of morals. Rather, the actions of humankind spring from the application of common, familiar sentiments, such as 'resentment of injuries', 'self-love' and the 'passion between the sexes' (Hume, 1975, p.22). To quote Hume:

> It is universally acknowledged that there is a great uniformity among the actions of men, in all nations and ages, and that human nature remains still the same, in its principles and operations. The same motives always produce the same actions: The same events follow the same causes. Ambition, avarice, self-love, vanity, friendship, generosity, public spirit: these passions, mixed in various degrees, and distributed through society, have been, from the beginning of all the world, and still are, the source of all the actions and enterprises, which have ever been observed among mankind. Would you know the sentiments, inclinations, and course of life of the Greeks and Romans? Study well the temper and actions of the French and English. (Hume, 1975, p.83) [12]

What a contrast Hume makes to Locke, Dubos or Montesquieu! There are general laws of human nature; there are laws of human motivation.

Hume allowed that these universally shared sentiments result in different norms in different societies. This is partly because different circumstances give the same norm different utilities. 'Inflexible rigour', for example, is more useful in a war-like society than in a 'polite' one. An additional cause of variation in norms is that sentiments conflict with one another: 'useful' sentiments will sometimes conflict with 'agreeable' ones. The difficulty of their reconciliation will make for some countries leaning too much on one side, and others too much on the other.[13] Hume's conclusion logically follows: varying behaviours are explicable in terms of these constant motives set in the context of varying circumstances.[14] Hume's vindication of a suprahistorical and supranational human nature was significant for economics, which has placed at its centre the supranational ahistorical concept of economic man. Hume's model of human behaviour helped set the stage for this ahistorical, supranational conception.

Having reconciled the superficial diversity of humankind with its underlying uniformity, Hume's next step was to discover the underlying laws of human nature. Hume pursued that object as an empiricist. As an empiricist he recommended that we restrict ourselves to the plain and apparent. 'The simplest and most obvious cause which can there be assigned for any phenomenon, is probably the true one' (Hume, 1975, p.299). As a believer in the existence of uniformity underlying superficial variety he recommended that generalizations be based on a broad range of experience. Hasty generalizations from narrow experience would give a false significance to superficial movements. Hume's hypothetical 'gloomy Yorkshireman' who predicts, on the basis of his calculations, that Yorkshire would soon be drained of specie is intended to be an illustration of that error, and shows that Hume was well aware of the frailty of precipitate extrapolations of political arithmeticians. His intention in writing 'Of the Balance of Trade', he said, was 'to remove people's errors, who are apt, from *chimerical calculations*, to imagine they are losing their specie, ...' (Hume, 1969, volume 1, p.144).[15]

The need for experience which is both plain and broadly based suggested to Hume that the Science of Man should focus its attention on the experiences of everyday life. So daily experience, already a touchstone in Mandeville, becomes something of fundamental importance to Hume. Attention to this daily experience will yield factual generalizations; such as that all men resent injury. These generalizations are all immediately and directly verified by 'daily experience'; they are all on the surface; there is no profound reasoning. These factual generalizations constitute Hume's general principles.

Having established an empirical foundation for general principles of human nature, Hume then advanced one step further. He proposed that these general principles could be deductively manipulated to provide predictions about the general course of things.

The puzzle about this last step is that Hume often warned that deductive logic is too subtle a tool for the clumsy human mind. 'The ... scientific method, where a general abstract principle is first established, and is afterwards branched out into a variety of inferences and conclusions, may be more perfect in itself, but suits less the imperfection of human nature, and is a common source of illusion ...' (Hume, 1975, p.174). 'It is easy', Hume warns, 'for a profound philosopher to commit a mistake in his subtile reasonings' (Hume, 1975, p.7).

But Hume also approved the use of deductive systems in certain situations. He explains those situations in what amounts to a methodological preface to his economic essays (Hume, 1987, pp.253-5). Those prefatory remarks are concerned with the appropriate element of reason in making a case for some conclusion. Hume claimed that the appropriate amount of deductive reasoning depends on whether the conclusion of the argument concerns the particular course of things or the general course of things. If it is the particular course of things then the 'natural, easy and shallow' reckoning of the great part of mankind was recommended, since deductive logic would come to grief by the neglect of some unknown circumstance. But deductive reasoning will not fail if the conclusion of the argument concerns the general course of things.

> When we reason upon *general* subjects, one may justly affirm, that our speculations can scarcely ever be too fine, provided they be just .... General reasonings seem intricate ... But however intricate they may seem, it is certain that general principles, if just and sound, must always prevail in the general course of things, though they may fail in particular cases; and it is the chief business of philosophers to regard the general course of things. I may add, that it is also the chief business of politicians; especially in the domestic government of the state, where the public good, which ought to be their object, depends on the concurrence of a multitude of causes. (Hume, 1987, p.254)

Hume evidently believed that a kind of 'law of averages' was in operation in which disturbances netted themselves out. In his own words, the general inclination of a society may be compared to a bias in a die: the bias 'may not appear in a few throws, [but] will certainly prevail in a great number' (Hume, 1987, p.112). Deductive reasoning could identify the 'bias' in a society's affairs.

With this justification laid down, Hume the empiricist was free to unbind his deductive reasonings from his empiricist strictures, and fill his pages on human affairs with deductive systems of his own devising. In the *Treatise of Human Nature*, for example, Hume attempted to arrive at knowledge of the human mind merely by working out the implications of a few psychological postulates (Hume, 1911, volume 2, p.54). He also provided theoretical arguments in favour of the money neutrality of the nominal rate of interest, and the self-equilibrating nature of the balance of trade.

In summary, Hume rescued deductivism, 'theory' and general reasonings from the place from which they had been so rudely shaken by Lockeans. He did this by:

1. Proofing the existence of general principles of human nature against their destruction by an accumulation of 'travellers' tales'.
2. Arguing that deductive systems based on generalizations will yield predictions which are true in general.
3. Distinguishing empirically based general principles from the discredited productions of dogmatists and 'profound philosophers'.

The third point is the most important and deserves some amplification. Hume, in keeping with the empiricist spirit of his day, expressly rejected the suggestion of profound philosophers that theory is somehow informative, or 'guiding', beyond experience (as the expression 'Theory tells us ...' would insinuate). Hume disdained the suggestion that 'theory' is somehow a source of knowledge different from experience: it is to regard theory as a kind of revealed religion. Hume sharply distinguishes his conception of theory from this. To Hume general principles are nothing more than general experience.

Hume's stress on the factuality of general principles led him to reject the distinction between *a priori* and *a posteriori*.

Nothing is more usual than for writers, even, on *moral*, *political* or *physical* subjects to distinguish between *reason* and *experience*, and to suppose, that these species of argumentation are entirely different from one another. But notwithstanding that this distinction be thus universally received, both in the active and speculative scenes of life, I shall not scruple to pronounce, that it is, at bottom, erroneous, at least, superficial. (Hume, 1975, p.43)

Hume claimed the distinction between *a priori* and *a posteriori* is superficial because sciences which are the result of mere reasoning will be found to terminate 'in some general principle or conclusion, for which we can assign no reason but observation and experience' (Hume, 1975, p.44). Hume illustrated the point by comparing *a posteriori* and *a priori* reasonings about the consequences of allowing arbitrary power to monarchs: 'The history of a Tiberius or a Nero makes us dread a like tyranny, were our monarchs freed from the restraints of laws and senates: But the observation of any fraud or cruelty in private life is sufficient, with the aid of a little thought, to give us the same apprehension; ... In both cases, it is experience which is ultimately the foundation of our inference and conclusion' (Hume, 1975, p.44).

By insisting on the empirical foundation of general principles, Hume was rebutting the Lockean presumption that principles must be worthless because they are *a priori*. To Hume, the *a priori* is empirical too. Therefore, to Hume, there could be no genuine *epistemological* dispute between Lockeans and the users of general principles. The real dispute between the advocates of general principles and Lockeans is not epistemological; it is metaphysical. To the advocates of general principles complexity is only the appearance overlaying uniformity; to Lockeans it is fundamental.

A sceptic is entitled to wonder to what extent Hume followed his own method of general experience. For while he sometimes displays a masterful sweep over a broad array of facts (for example, his 'Of the Populousness of Ancient Nations'), his most effective contributions to economic doctrine seem *a priori* in a traditional Cartesian manner. His demonstration of money neutrality, for example, begins with the proposition that the quantity theory of money is a 'maxim almost self-evident' (Hume, 1987, p.290). To what extent did his methodology of general principles by experience disguise a Cartesian methodology?

5.3 Hume's theoretical history

Hume's attempt to dissolve the *a priori/a posteriori* distinction, and to make general reasonings consistent with empiricism, was strongly influential on the English economists of the early 19th century. To give one example, John Stuart Mill in discussing the method proper to political economy, sought to illustrate the difference between *a priori* and *a posteriori* reasonings as follows:

> Suppose, for example, that the question were, whether absolute kings were likely to employ the powers of government for the welfare or for the oppression of their subjects. The practicals would endeavour to determine the question by a direct induction from the conduct of particular despotic monarchs, as testified by history. The theorists would refer the question to be decided by the test not solely of our experience of kings, but of our experience of men. (Mill, 1844, p.142)

This is comparison drawn directly from Hume.

The 'theoretical method' of the 20th century, by contrast, would not find much in common with Hume's method of general principles by experience. His attempt to legitimate general principles and theorizing by founding them on nothing but experience would today be seen as neglecting several important characteristics of theories.

First, there is a *hypothetical* element in theories, which has been greatly stressed in 20th century philosophy of science. To many philosophers of science the hypothetical nature of theories is irremediable; it is in their very nature. Hume seems neglectful of this hypothetical element. It is true that in Book II of the *Treatise*, in the best hypothetico-deductive manner, Hume announced seven 'experiments to confirm' his 'system' of psychology. But the very use of the word 'confirm' separates him from the 20th century tendency to stress hypotheticality. Hume was only remaining true to his empiricism in begrudging the hypothetical element in theories, but at the cost, great or small, of most general reasoning.

Second, Hume seems to be neglectful of the role of the *ideal* element in theories. No lines are ever exactly straight, no firm ever exactly maximizes profits, and almost all exact general claims are false. But ideal entities, such as the profit maximizing, firm play a central role in economic theory. How to chose the 'best' ideal, and how to cope with its inevitable falsehood, is a critical problem for economic theory.

Third, the *instrumental* aspect of general principles is ignored. Hume's interpretation of belief as a kind of custom would have provided a foundation for an instrumentalist approach; the notion of belief as a 'custom' and theory as a 'rule' are clearly congruent. In addition, his metaphysics claimed that many familiar conceptions, (such as 'substance' and 'cause and effect') are but 'fictions', 'illusions' and 'imaginary' (for example Hume, 1969, p.94). This doctrine would also have provided a lead to the notion of theory as a useful fiction. But he can barely be said to have pursued this notion. Vaihinger (1924) in *The Philosophy of 'As If'* correctly points out that Hume, in contrast to a true instrumentalist, does not stress the utility of the fictions he identifies (Vaihinger, 1924, pp.99, 156).

But if Hume's approach neglects the hypothetical, the ideal and the instrumental, which loom so large in current 'theoretical method', his treatment of the theoretical does have a surviving progeny in the practice of 'theoretical history'. Theoretical history may be defined as history which is concerned to explain the general tendencies of historical change (rather than particular events), by way of other (supposedly) general principles of human nature.[16]

Hume's *Natural History of Religion* is an example of theoretical history. So is his essay 'Of the Rise and the Progress of the Arts and Sciences' (Hume, 1987). The method of theoretical history also coloured many 'actual' histories of the Enlightenment, including to some degree Hume's six-volume *History of England*, and the economic history of the *Wealth of Nations*. In the opinion of Carl Becker, and many other 20th century historians, even this 'actual' Enlightenment history was not interested in the diversity of mankind's experience; it was interested in explaining its general character; they were searching for 'general man': 'Man in general, like the economic man, was a being that did not exist in the world of time and place, but in the conceptual world, and he could be found only by abstracting from all men in all times and all places those qualities all men shared' (Becker, 1932, p.99).

This stylized, abstracting general history lives today. But not among historians. It is sometimes practised by sociologists (e.g. Hall, 1986), and, on occasion, by economists. Rostow's *Stages of Economic*

Growth is one example of hypothetical history. An attractive example of the genre has been furnished by John Hicks in *A Theory of Economic History*. Hicks compares his 'theory of history' to that of Marx, but it bears a much closer resemblance to the histories of many Enlightenment *philosophes*. Hicks and Enlightenment 'history' share the preoccupation with generalities; he describes his task as an inquiry 'which must proceed in general terms-the more general the better' (Hicks, 1969, p.6). Particular persons or events are not addressed; they are irrelevant. They cannot explain tendencies, which must be explained by reference to the typical and the average: a claim exactly anticipated by Hume in 1742 in 'Of the Rise and the Progress of the Arts and Sciences' (Hume, 1987, pp.111-3).

This theoretical history, whatever its value, is probably the true inheritor of Hume's general yet empirical outlook.

5.4 Hume on passion's servant

Mandeville and Hutcheson had coupled uniformitarianism to empiricism, and Hume bound the two doctrines together more firmly. In what amounted to a parallel procedure, Hume also reinforced Mandeville's and Hutcheson's union of their optimism about a world order with their pessimism about human rationality.

Hutcheson and Mandeville had believed reason exerted little influence in human affairs, but they also felt no larger role was needed: a functioning world order existed even though humankind was not rational. Locke agreed that reason had small influence in human affairs, but was inclined to think it should have more in some matters. In contrast, Dubos believed reason had small influence in human affairs, but felt it still had too much influence, since he repudiated almost all claims of reason to rule human affairs. Put crudely, the difference between Hutcheson, Locke and Dubos on reason is the difference between 'reason does not rule, but need not'; 'reason does not rule, but (sometimes) should' and 'reason does (sometimes) rule, but should not'.

Hume's position was different again; it was essentially 'reason does not rule and cannot rule'. So while Dubos said that reason could not hold the throne in human affairs legitimately, and Hutcheson and Locke said reason did not in fact hold the throne, Hume said reason could never hold the throne, either legitimately or illegitimately. This was partly because, as a matter of pure logic, a passion could never be in conflict with reason. Even very peculiar passions, such as to prefer a lesser good for oneself over a larger one, could not constitute in itself a conflict with reason (Hume, 1911, volume 2, p.128). Reason and passion had entirely different domains, and could never cross-swords or rule the other. Hume here was adding logical force to the claim of Dubos that passion is a legitimate criterion of judgement in its own right and need not answer to reason. Hume's attitude to time preference illustrates his position that reason and passions could not be in conflict. Earlier, Locke had said that it was the weak and narrow constitutions of our minds that made for our preference for present over future pleasures: time preference was an intellectual failing. Hume, by contrast, said it was an 'abuse of terms' to suppose the preference between present and future pleasures was 'the determinations of pure reason and reflection'. A passion for present pleasures could not be said to be against reason.

But, although reason could never do battle with passion, Hume did not deprive reason of all claims on passion. He allows a passion can be contrary to reason when the passion 'chooses means insufficient for the designed end ...'(Hume, 1911, volume 2, p.128).[17] So reason, it seems, may still provide the 'means sufficient for the designed end'. Reason is reduced from king to councillor. Passions give ends and valuations, and reason only supplies the means sufficient for those ends. Reason becomes passion's obedient servant. This appears entirely congruent with the modern neoclassical viewpoint.

However Hume's position on the use of means to obtain ends (i.e. instrumental rationality) is distinguishable from the neoclassical viewpoint. One distinguishing feature is that Hume did not believe that we always do choose means sufficient for the designed end. 'Mankind are, in all ages, caught by the same baits: The same tricks played over and over again, still trepan them' (Hume, 1987, p.363). Hume's attitude to intertemporal choice also illustrates how his position on instrumental rationality differs from the modern neoclassical. Although Hume agrees with the modern neoclassical that it is not irrational to prefer present to future pleasures, Hume was also strongly of the opinion that the tendency of humankind to give priority to present over the future pleasures was responsible for 'lasting shame and sorrow', 'disorder, repentance, and misery' (Hume, 1975, p.239, also 1987, p.38). Hume was evidently doubtful that in choosing between the present and the future 'we choose means sufficient for the designed end' of happiness. Thus having presented a concept of instrumental rationality which is entirely acceptable to the modern neoclassical, Hume now scoffs at the notion that human beings are instrumentally rational.

But the contrast of Hume's position with the neoclassical vision of the role of reason extends further. Hume's attack on reason did not end with the proposition that reason cannot conflict with passion. It did not end with reason being reduced to councillor, or even an unreliable councillor. His epistemology led him to almost conclude that reason was virtually powerless to do anything.

The critical feature of Hume's epistemology was its audacious doubts about the possibility of knowledge. Hume had several lines of argument in favour of his scepticism. He adopted the familiar empiricist contention that our knowledge can only be of surface appearances, and therefore underlying realities are hidden. Hume also sharpened ancient rationalist scepticism regarding the value of generalizations based on experience. His famed analysis of induction concluded that the fact that bread has nourished in the past gives no reason to believe that the loaf before us will nourish now. In addition, Hume developed novel scepticisms about the knowledge of causes.

Taken at face value Hume's sceptical contentions would lead to the conclusion that there were no good grounds to believe anything 'beyond the present testimony of our senses, or the records of our memory' (Hume, 1975, p.26). Hume did allow that all philosophical and subtle reasonings are open to doubt, including sceptical ones (Hume, 1911, volume 1, p.253). But Hume challenged the world to provide rational justifications for our beliefs about the future and causation, and was confident no one had succeeded in meeting this challenge.

Hume's conclusion that a search for rational justifications leads to an impasse of doubts has implications for human beings if they are to survive. Human beings must be active, and not philosophical; they must feel and act, and not require justifications, for no rational justifications are known. So not only is reason not necessary to our survival (Hutcheson's doctrine); it is actually hostile to our survival.

With reason a positive hindrance to our survival, Hume can dispense with the notion of humankind as logically rational, or philosophic. Hume rejected the Cartesian notion that the intellect was essential to humankind, and thereby distinguished humankind from animals. That reason is inessential to humanity perhaps encouraged Hume's claim, with Locke and against Leibniz, that there is a 'great difference in human understandings'. In the same vein, Hume maintains we have no love of truth in itself (Hume, 1911, volume 2, p.157).

Hume also attacked the integrity of the intellect we do possess. The human mind is not a coherent whole, but a 'heap of contradictions'. He threw doubt on whether the intellect even existed autonomously from passions at all. Reason and passion and senses coexist, intermingled and indistinct in a continuum: '... all probable reasoning is nothing but a species of sensation. It is not solely in poetry and music we must follow our taste and sentiment, but likewise in philosophy' (Hume, 1911, volume 2, p.105). This intermingling is actually welcome, says Hume. What is best is an alloy of reason and passion: 'Where reason is lively, and mixes itself with some propensity, it ought to be assented to' (Hume, 1911, volume 1, p.255). The notion that philosophy and poetry are on the same continuum was plainly influential on Smith.

Since reason is not necessary, and is indeed hostile, to our survival, Hume inferred that nature must have provided some principles other than reason to preserve us from perishing (Hume, 1975, p.106). These principles are imagination, habit and the 'passions'. It is due to our *imaginative principles* that we believe, on the basis of experience, that fire burns and water drowns. 'Animals ... are not guided in these inferences by reasoning: Neither are children: Neither are the generality of mankind, in their ordinary actions and conclusions: Neither are philosophers themselves ...' (Hume, 1975, p.106). If the 'imaginative principles' on which our beliefs are based were eliminated then 'human nature must immediately perish and go to ruin' (Hume, 1911, volume 1, p.216). It is to *custom* that humankind continues to maintain valuable social conventions: property, money, the state, various norms. These institutions arose slowly from experience and are preserved by habit, rather than reason. It is also to habit and custom that we owe a good measure of our beliefs about causation and the resemblance of the future to the past. And it is to *passions* of sociability, restlessness and 'self-love' that the human race maintains and reproduces itself.

So philosophy is no basis for survival: the basis is rather imagination, habit and the passions. We no longer survive in spite of our customs, passions and fancies, but because of them. For it is only custom, imagination and passion which can supply the means sufficient for our ends.

This annihilation of reason as a basis of survival leads to one of Hume's great paradoxical turns, for this annihilation was turned by Hume against pessimists such as John Locke. By adopting a position of the necessary powerlessness of reason Hume was undermining despair over the absence of reason. Since reason cannot rule, one may obviously conclude that it does not rule; in this conclusion Hume was siding with Locke. But since reason cannot rule, it makes no sense to say it should rule; in this conclusion he was opposing the pessimism of Locke.

Correspondingly, Hume did not despair over the power of custom, as John Locke did. For Hume did not suppose that the customs, imagination and passions which supply the means for our ends are 'irrational'. They were non-rational, certainly. But they were not irrational. For these customs etc. to be irrational would require the existence of a rational alternative, and no rational alternative existed. So to Hume the 'not rational' did not mean the same thing as 'irrational', 'passion' does not mean the same thing as 'unreason', and a 'passion-infested world' need not be an 'irrationality-infested world'. One illustration of this difference between Hume and Locke is provided by their different analyses of customary behaviour originating in the chance association of ideas (see Locke, 1959, II, xxxiii). To Locke such behaviour was not rational, and Hume agreed. But whereas Locke assumed this non-rational behaviour was irrational, Hume did not. So while Locke was pessimistic about the impact of customary behaviour, Hume was more optimistic.

Looking forward, Hume's position is a challenge to both neoclassical economics and its critics. It is a challenge to neoclassicals who claim, for example, that stock market behaviour is 'rational': to Hume such market behaviour is not rational; it is non-rational. But his position is equally a challenge to critics of neoclassical economics, who claim, for example, that stock market behaviour is 'irrational': to Hume such market behaviour is not irrational; it is non-rational. Hume was saying the human conduct is beyond considerations of rationality and irrationality.

5.5 Conclusion

Hume reinforced the synthesis of rationalism and anti-rationalism wrought by Mandeville and Hutcheson. Hume was, as they were, empiricist and uniformitarian. But unlike them, he provided a plausible reconciliation of the two. Hume argued that empirically established general principles could explain the variety observed in human conduct.

Hume's defence of uniformitarianism had important consequences. By insisting on the factual nature of general principles he gave confidence to the economic theorists of the 18th century, and later. By asserting the empirical foundation of *a priori* reasonings he rehabilitated general principles and their deductive exploitation.

Hume also strengthened Mandeville and Hutcheson's synthesis of a rationalist metaphysical optimism with an anti-rationalist pessimism about human rationality. To Hume it is human non-rationality which actually makes optimism possible, since humanity owes its survival to its non-rational behaviour.

Notes

1 Korsmeyer (1977, p.205) points out a difference between Voltaire's Dr Pangloss and Leibniz. Dr Pangloss's optimism was empirically based, while Leibniz's optimism was based on *a priori* reasonings.
2 Montesquieu's doctrines had many sources. See Fletcher, 1939 and Shackleton, 1955.
3 This homage may be in part a redress for Montesquieu's sharp rebuttal of Dubos's history of the Franks (Montesquieu, 1989, pp.659-68).
4 Geographical data was another material condition with which Montesquieu and Dubos shared a great interest. About half of the pages devoted to commerce in the *Esprit des Lois* are taken up with a long geographical history of commerce contained in Book 21.
5 Shaftesbury: 'See there the mutual dependency of things! the relation of one to another ... the order, union and coherence of the whole!' (quoted in Myers, 1972, p.166). Dubos, too, wrote of the 'linking and reciprocal dependence which exists between all the parts of the material world' (quoted in Caramaschi, 1959, p.235).
6 Mandeville claimed that desirable social outcomes may be produced by the impact of contrary forces. 'I would compare the Body Politick ... to a Bowl of Punch. Avarice

should be the Souring and Prodigality the Sweetning of it. The Water I would call Ignorance ...; while Wisdom ... should be an Equivalent to Brandy. I don't doubt but a ... dull Stranger ... if he was to taste the several Ingredients apart, would think it impossible they should make any tolerable Liquor. Yet Experience teaches us, that the Ingredients I named judiciously mixt, will make an excellent Liquor ...' (Mandeville, 1924, volume 1, p.105).

7 Stark (1960, p.20) drew attention to the number of times 'balance' appears in Montesquieu (Montesquieu, 1949, volume 2, pp.603,968,977), but denied any significance to these appearances. In Stark's judgement, the term 'balance' is no more than a 'convenient mode of expression' of an early Cartesianism which the mature Montesquieu discarded. It is maintained here that it is a manifestation of Montesquieu's view that the world is characterized by a structure of interdependence, a position which is antithetical to the Cartesian notion of a structure of hierarchy.

8 Spiegel (1975) credits Boisguillebert (1646-1714) with the first use of the word 'equilibrium' in an economic context.

9 There is, however, no automatic equilibrium. In a passage which may remind the reader of Mandeville, Condillac states that the politician must establish social equilibrium, by ensuring that the public interest coincides with the private interest of each social class (Condillac, 1947, volume 1, p.208).

10 Turgot extended the notion of a structure of mutual interdependence to include the structure of knowledge. He traced how the structure of knowledge has evolved from a structure of hierarchy to a structure of mutual interdependence: 'The different sciences, confined at first to a small number of simple principles, common to all, can no longer be envisaged as other than separate when progress has extended and complicated them: but a progress still more great unites them, owing to the discovery of that mutual dependence of all truths which, in linking them together, illuminates each by the other ...' (Turgot, 1913, volume 1, p.235).

11 But Hume and Montesquieu would draw different inferences from a foreigner's 'travellers' tale' of the West. Montesquieu would infer 'We would look strange, therefore we are strange. We are as strange as the foreign world'. Hume would infer, 'We would look strange, therefore strange looks deceive. The foreign world is as normal as us.'

12 See also Hume, 1911, volume 2, p.116.

13 The explanation of the variety of human conduct by reference to the variety of optimization errors had also been advanced in Maupertuis's *Essai de Philosophie Morale* of 1749. Was Maupertuis indebted to Hume on this and other matters? Cassirer claimed that the similarities between the *Essai de Cosmologie* of 1750 and Hume's *Treatise of Human Nature* of 1739 are so considerable that Maupertuis must have read the *Treatise*. If true, this would constitute a rare piece of influence of the *Treatise* on 18th century thought. Certainly, Maupertuis judged Hume to be 'one of the greatest men in England' (Oake, 1940 p.81). But Oake argues that the author of the *Essai* had not read the *Treatise*: any similarities must owe themselves to the common origin of the two thinkers' ideas.

14 'The Rhine flows north, the Rhone south; yet both spring from the *same* mountain, and are also actuated in the opposite directions, by the *same* principle of gravity. The different inclinations of ground, on which they run, cause all the difference of their courses' (Hume, 1975, p.333).

15 Our italics.

16 It may appear that Hume was trying to expound a sort of 'ideal' history, in which the path of human history in the absence of the 'disturbances' is outlined. But this

appearance is misleading. Hume was trying to explain trends or tendencies in human life, as one may try to explain the bias in a die. The tendency of human life is a compound of all events, just as the bias of a die is a compound of all throws of the die. The tendency with which Hume is concerned does not ignore the class of 'disturbing' events: it is made up of all of events.

17 Hume added 'even then it is not the passion, properly speaking, which is unreasonable, but the judgment'(Hume, 1911, volume 2, p.128).

6. Condillac, Turgot and the well-made language of science

David Hume had restored the role of general principles in human affairs by asserting they had a firmly empirical basis. By this logic, David Hume, the philosopher of the *a posteriori* became the economist of the *a priori*.

This contribution of Hume to economic method was paralleled in the work of Étienne Bonnot de Condillac (1715-80). Both were empirical in ambition, and yet appreciated the weakness of a purely Lockean empiricism. But whereas Hume sought to reform Lockean empiricism, Condillac discarded it. So both Condillac and Hume encouraged an epistemological shift from Lockean empiricism to more 'theoretical' approaches to economics. But the shift of Condillac was greater.

The irony in this is that Condillac has been seen as little more than a paraphraser of Locke. In truth, there is a sharp incongruity between the intentions and achievements of E.B. de Condillac. Setting out to strengthen Locke's doctrine of human knowledge, he finished by undermining it. Beginning with the task of completing Locke, he ended by reviving Leibniz. Draining Locke's philosophy of its empiricism, he infused it with rationalism.

Condillac's revival of rationalism in decent empirical dress lent itself well to abstract economic theory. The result is seen in Condillac's *Le Commerce et le Gouvernement Considérés Relativement l'un à l'autre* (1776). This reformed rationalism was shared by Condillac's lifelong philosophic ally, A.R.J. Turgot (1727-81).[1] It is plainly manifested in Turgot's *Réflexions sur la Formation et la Distribution des Richesses* (1766).

This chapter examines Condillac's 'rationalist empiricism', and then examines the influence it had on the economics of Condillac and Turgot.

6.1 Condillac and Turgot on human understanding

Condillac was a polymath whose learning covered economics, philosophy, psychology, physics and history. His reputation is based on his epistemology which he developed in the *Essai sur l'Origine des Connaissances Humaines* (1746), the *Traité des Systèmes* (1749), the *Traité des Sensations* (1754) and *La Logique* (1780). The net result of Condillac's epistemology was to elevate conception over perception; the abstract over the particular; deduction over induction; and to stress the necessity of hypothesis and method. He did all this while seeing himself as an adversary of rationalists, such as Descartes, and as the improver of the doctrines of John Locke. All his 'improvements' of Locke, however, tended to rationalism.

Consider the role of the sensual basis of human knowledge. In sympathy with John Locke, Condillac repeatedly states that sense reports constitute the sole origins of knowledge. But to Condillac 'raw' sensation is not informative. To make use of it one must decompose sense reports and abstract from them.

We must decompose 'raw' sensation, said Condillac, because our senses provide us with only sensual complexes: the view out the window, for example. To make use of them we must decompose these aggregates into their elements, and compare and relate the elements. This decomposition, comparison and relation comprises reasoning. So reasoning 'merely' consists of an articulation of our sensations. In making this equivalence Condillac was, like Hume and Dubos, seeking to blur the distinction between reason and sensation: reasoning is 'reduced' to sensation (Condillac, 1947, volume 2, p.385). This is all part of Condillac's wholehearted psychological anti-rationalism, which he shared with Hume and Dubos. There is, however, an ambiguity in the equation of sensation and reason. By 'sensualizing' reason, Condillac was at the same time 'intellectualizing' the senses.

Humankind must also abstract from raw sensation, says Condillac, because of the 'obscurity and uncertainty of sensible ideas':

When I say that all our knowledge comes from the senses, we must not forget that it is only as much as it is derived from the clear and distinct ideas that they contain. It is clear that I have an idea of a triangle even though I cannot be certain that the object that I see and touch is indeed triangular. Thus, in order to dispel the obscurity and uncertainty of our sensory ideas we have only to consider them abstracted from objects: then we will find in our sensations exact ideas of size and shape .... From other abstractions we make we will discover ... all of the moral sciences. (Condillac, 1947, volume 1, p.721)

In the above we see Condillac, a 'Lockean', making an attack on sense perceptions which is of great antiquity: they are obscure and uncertain. Our conception of a triangle, by contrast, is certain. Condillac was resorting to the basic rationalist criterion of knowledge: that ideas be *clear and distinct*. And, in sympathy with this, he hinted at resurrecting the Lockean suggestion that morals can be demonstrated, like geometry. 'Moral philosophy', he noted hopefully, does not have the problem of obscure ideas: 'How great soever the variety with which the causes of pleasure and pain affect men of different constitutions, it is sufficient that the meaning of these words, *pleasure* and *pain,* is so well fixed that nobody can mistake it' (Condillac, 1971, p.310).

Condillac held that abstraction from sense reports is also made necessary by the incapacity of our minds to absorb all the infinity of particulars which the senses present.[2] The human mind must drop some of the details of these particulars, and treat certain particulars as identical. The human mind must devise abstract categories (tree, fruit) in which diverse particulars are placed. These categories of generalization do not arise from the meditations of philosophers, but are based solely on the usefulness to our survival. Everybody who survives must have a 'system' which guides their decisions in daily life, whether they be philosopher or plebeian (Condillac, 1947, volume 1, p.216). In Condillac's opinion, a person cannot even speak without making abstractions; they cannot think without deploying genera (Condillac, 1947, volume 1, p.216; Condillac, 1979, p.249). Abstraction and systems (or 'theory') are an essential part of the human mind.

Therefore to Condillac not all 'systems' are bad; some are good and some are bad. The bad systems are *philosophical* systems. To make his point against these philosophical systems, Condillac supplied a detailed critique of the systems of the Descartes, Malebranche, Spinoza and Leibniz.[3] The good system is that given by nature. It arises 'naturally' out of habit and imitation, and our habits and imitation serve our needs much better than philosophers. To Condillac 'errors begin when Nature ceases to warn us of our mistakes' (Condillac, 1979, p.57). This disdain for the cogitations of profound philosophers, this respect for habit and custom, are entirely one with Hume and Dubos. What was new was his representation of habit and custom as a system.

Turgot shared Condillac's mixed attitude to 'systems' or theories. Everyone who is not a madman must have a 'system', says Turgot. But some are good and some are bad. The bad system is a 'philosophical' system, which consists of

> ... those arbitrary suppositions with the help of which it is attempted to explain all phenomena and which actually explain them all equally, because they do not explain any; that lack of observation, that overhasty reliance on obscure analogies by which a particular fact is rashly transformed into a general principle, and the whole is judged by a superficial glance at a part; that blind presumption which relates all it does not know to the little it knows; that blind presumption ... which wants to know all, to explain all, arrange all, and which, ignorant of the inexhaustible variety of nature, claims to subjugate it to its arbitrary and limited methods, and tries to circumscribe the infinite in order to embrace it. (Quoted in Groenewegen, 1977, p.38)

A good system, said Turgot, is 'an opinion adopted after mature consideration, supported by proofs and consistent in its consequences ... a settled opinion resulting from a chain of observations ...'. In a surprising Malebranchian flourish, Turgot adds that the holder of a good system 'is inwardly convinced of the truth, and deduces consequences from it with the rigour of exact logic' (quoted in Groenewegen, 1977, p.38). Turgot's equivocal attitude to systems is reflected in his maxim: 'The first step is to find a system; the second is to become disgusted with it' (Turgot, 1913, volume 1, p.315).

With this rehabilitation of systems went a rehabilitation of hypothesis. To Condillac hypotheses are 'not only useful, but necessary' in mathematics and astronomy (Condillac, 1947, volume 1, p.203). 'It is rare that one arrives immediately at the evidence: in all sciences and all arts one begins with a kind of groping' (Condillac, 1947, volume 2, p.412). 'It is necessary to make suppositions, it is necessary to make errors; and these sorts of errors are useful because by indicating the observations which remain to be made, they lead to the truth' (Condillac, 1947, volume 1, p.645).

Turgot shared Condillac's esteem of hypothesis. Hypothesis compensates for the limits of our senses. 'Observer of the Universe, his senses in showing him the effects leave him ignorant of the causes

...' (Turgot, 1913, volume 1, p.219). Many empiricists would not disagree with this. But Turgot parted from pure empiricism in his belief that hypothesis provides a ready remedy for this ignorance.

> Thus, in order to divine the cause of an effect when our impressions do not present it to us, it is necessary to imagine one; it is necessary to check several hypotheses and try them. But how does one check them? It is by developing the consequences of each hypothesis and comparing it with the facts. If all the facts that one predicts in consequence of the hypothesis, are found in nature precisely as the hypothesis requires, this conformity, which cannot happen by chance, becomes the verification ... (Turgot, 1913, volume 1, p.314)[4]

Thus by the hypothetico-deductive method we advance to knowledge. Good hypotheses enlighten, while bad hypotheses are rejected. 'Hypotheses are not destructive: all that are false destroy themselves' (Turgot, 1913, volume 1, p.315). Turgot's attitude is reminiscent of falsificationism in the 20th century. This is no accident. Falsificationism, like the doctrines of Turgot and Condillac, is a product of the intersection of empiricist and rationalist aspirations (see Gellner, 1992, pp.105-09).

6.2 The well-made language of science

But in the minds of Condillac and Turgot the role of hypothesis in scientific achievement stands in only a distant second place to the tool which makes all science possible: language.

Condillac claimed that the crucial operations of decomposition and abstraction of sense reports depend greatly on the existence of symbols. One must give signs to the elements of sensual aggregates which one seeks to decompose; and one must give signs to those complexes which our abstractions contrive. So it is by means of signs that we move from consciousness to reflection. Imagine, Condillac asked, attempting without signs, numerals or symbols, the arithmetical operations (the ultimate exercise in abstraction and decomposition). Without mathematical language there would be no mathematical reasoning. And without ordinary language there would be no ordinary reason. By this line of argument Condillac arrived at one of his most remarkable doctrines: that science is nothing more than a 'well-made language'. It is only by language being ill-made that a subject is stopped from resembling algebra in its exactness and certainty: 'If some sciences do not seem to permit of demonstration it is because one is accustomed to speaking them before having made a language for them' (Condillac, 1979, p.301). Condillac evidently believed that he had discovered in language the 'right method', that algorithm of producing knowledge, which earlier rationalists had sought in mathematics or axiomatics. So Condillac's programme for the advance of science amounts to the reform of our language, and the elimination of ideas loosely linked to symbols ('unfixed ideas', 'vague principles').

In *Réflexions sur les Langues*, written about 1751 (Turgot, 1913, volume 1, p.347), Turgot expressed a similar view about the vital role of language in the advance of science. In a manner reminiscent of Condillac, he wrote of signs as lifting us from sensations to metaphysics. He recommended the study of a 'well-made language' as the best logic. He later made conceptual analysis an important test of the worth of any thinking. For example, in 1773 Turgot justified his derision of Helvétius's *De L'Esprit* on the grounds that it had not 'a single idea analysed with accuracy, not a word defined with precision' (Turgot, 1913, volume 3, p.637). In a letter to Du Pont in 1771 Turgot grumbled that 'logic is not the strength of the *Economistes*. Their error is in general to want to advance too quickly and not to analyse the meaning of words with necessary diligence' (Turgot, 1913, volume 3, p.498).

It seems that in the minds of Condillac and Turgot, science reduces to a conceptual analysis based on 'clear and distinct' ideas. To 'empiricists' like Turgot and Condillac everything comes down to words. What a contrast Condillac and Turgot make to Locke and Mandeville, with their disdain of mere words, and talk and disputation! To Locke words were a 'mist' before our eyes, something to be cleared away to allow our senses to operate. To Condillac and Turgot they seem to be the very coin of thought.

What makes the position of Condillac unappealing to moderns is that the only propositions which are just a matter of words are 'analytic' propositions, or tautologies. But Condillac does not shy away from this implication of his position. In his later work the sentiment that everything comes down to words culminates in his doctrine that all true propositions are merely 'identical propositions', or definitional propositions, in which the words on the 'right hand side' of the identity expression make explicit what is implicit on the left hand side. In *De l'Art de Penser* of 1775 he writes:

> Every truth is an identical proposition. Indeed the proposition, *the gold is yellow, heavy, fusible etc.* is only true because I have formed a complex idea of gold which includes those qualities. In short, a proposition is only the development of a complex idea ... it limits itself to affirming that the same is the same. (Condillac, 1947, volume 1, p.748)

The domain of tautological truth is extended by Condillac to embrace entire scientific theories;

> A whole system may be no more than one and the same idea. If, in all the sciences, we could equally trace the origin of ideas, and grasp the true system of things, we would see how from one truth all the other truths are born, and we would find a concise expression of all what we know in this identical proposition: *the same is the same.* (Condillac, 1947, volume 1, p.749)

Here is a paradox! An empiricist who says that all science is mere tautology![5] Condillac puts this paradox to himself:

> Are the human sciences, therefore, no more than a collection of trivial propositions? Mathematics has been criticised in this way; but the criticism is groundless. A child learning to count thinks he has made a discovery the first time he realises that two and two makes four. He is not mistaken. It is for him. Although any true proposition is identical, it need not seem so to the person who notices, for the first time, the relationship of its component terms. On the contrary, it is an instructive proposition, a discovery. (Condillac, 1947, volume 1, p.748)

Condillac's peculiar doctrine that all truths are identical propositions had been entertained earlier by Leibniz (Leibniz, 1969, paper no 30). This may be more than coincidental. Condillac, despite his admonitions of profound philosophical systems, was strongly drawn to Leibniz's philosophy. The strength of this attraction became especially plain with the publication in 1980 of a paper on Leibniz's metaphysical system which Condillac had anonymously submitted in 1746 to the Berlin Academy (Condillac, 1980). In this paper Condillac demonstrates to his own satisfaction several of Leibniz's controversial metaphysical doctrines.

This notion of the identity of all truths had a reflection, or parallel, in the peculiar presumption of Condillac and Turgot that the factual base of science and the general principles of science were logically identical. They believed, in a Lockean fashion, that general principles just restated in summary form the known facts. Following Locke, they believed that, historically, the facts were discovered first, and then expressed in general principles (see Locke, 1959, IV, vii, 11). For example, Turgot claimed that geometry began with the measurement of fields, and that later these discoveries were summarized as general principles (Turgot, 1973, p.97). This assumption of the identity of principles and facts implies that one could equally make inferences from the general principles to the factual base, and from the factual base to general principles. Condillac compared this two-way process to going up and down the same valley. More concretely, Turgot said of geometry, 'in geometry ... these relationships are reciprocal; that one may infer the principle from the consequence and the consequence from the principle ...' (Turgot, 1973, p.97).

This attempt by Turgot and Condillac to dissolve the distinction between facts and principles has a parallel in Hume's attempt to dissolve the distinction between the *a posteriori* and the *a priori*. And, as with Hume, this apparently highly empiricist proposal was actually conducive to theory, since the doctrine implicitly assured its adherents that all that went by the name of 'theory' was in truth solid fact.

But the attitude of Turgot and Condillac to the relation between facts and principles can also be distinguished from that of Hume's. Hume never held that there was an identity between facts and principles, or that, in Turgot's words, 'one may infer the principle from the consequence and the consequence from the principle'. Needless to say, this claim of Turgot is utterly false: one cannot infer the principle from the consequence as one infers the consequence from the principle, and so on; there is not a unique correspondence between factual base and principles; the factual base is consistent with many different principles. This error betrays the fact that Turgot and Condillac wholly missed the distinction between inductive logic and deductive logic. They seemed to miss the whole problem of judging the most likely principles, given the factual base. Hume was alive to this problem, and it was to be a central concern of many later philosophers of science. It is little wonder Condillac's work received the scorn of later British empiricists such as J.S. Mill, who were concerned to develop the 'canons of induction' (see for example Mill, 1980, p.115).[6]

The alternative to deduction (or 'synthesis') which Condillac favoured was not induction but 'analysis'. But his theory of analysis was just another expression of his sentiment that discovery is a matter of making the implicit explicit.

Condillac developed the notion *l'analyse* at length in his three epistemological works: *La Logique*, *L'Origine des Connaissances Humaines*, and *Traité des Systèmes*. Condillac explains *l'analyse* by an example, which could have been drawn from a primer in algebra. Consider this problem:

Having some tokens in my two hands, if I move one from the right hand to the left, I will have as many in one as in the other; and if I move one from the left to the right, I will have twice as many in the latter.

He has these two statements recast into two simultaneous equations:

$$x - 1 = y + 1$$
$$x + 1 = 2y - 2$$

and solves them; $y = 5$, $x = 7$. This, to Condillac, is a paradigm of 'analysis'. Obviously the method of inference here is purely deductive. It is not the 'observo-inductive' method which we often associate with empiricism; there are no inductive leaps from particular to more embracing propositions: all the inferences are deductive; every conclusion is implicitly contained in the assumptions.

The vision underlying Condillac's 'analysis' is that all we want to know is implicitly in the facts at hand, and it is just a matter of making the implicit explicit. It is merely a matter of absorbing all the clues, and 'putting two and two together' like a detective, and deriving the answer which the clues were silently speaking the whole time. This outlook, that the world is a riddle waiting to be 'figured out', is a classic rationalist attitude. This outlook is, however, inadequate. The given facts are consistent with many different theories, that is, the given 'clues' have no single 'solution'. A fundamental challenge facing scientific inquiry is to discriminate among the many different solutions to the given set of clues.

In summary, one might say that Condillac and Turgot provide the spectacle of the fragile foreign body of Lockean empiricism being engulfed and assimilated by French rationalism.[7] Condillac and Turgot sifted out the anti-rationalist elements in Locke and developed the remaining rationalist elements. Locke, for example, had wished that ideas be 'clear and distinct'; and this rationalist element in Locke was pursued by Condillac and Turgot. Locke believed in the existence of necessary truths concerning 'nominal essences' and some 'real essences', and this notion was expanded by Condillac to embrace every truth. Locke had advanced the view that knowledge 'be nothing but the *perception of the connexion of and agreement, or disagreement and repugnancy of any of our ideas*' (Locke, 1959, IV, i, 1); Condillac concluded that science was nothing but conceptual analysis.

6.3 Condillac's well-made language of economics

The rationalist emphasis of Condillac and Turgot prepared the ground well for the development of economic theory, and one rather more starkly abstract than that which Hume's method favoured. We see this in the economic writings of Condillac and Turgot.

Condillac's contribution to economics consists of a single work: *Le Commerce et le Gouvernement Considérés Relativement l'un à l'autre*, published in 1776. In this he advances a utility theory of value, explains the gains from trade, and even hints at an imputation theory of factor pricing. Condillac in this work reveals himself as one of those writers who tempt historians to look forward rather than back.[8] His resources in this achievement are twofold: the subjectivist inheritance of Dubos and others, which had put passion rather than reason as the proper arbiter in human judgements; and the rationalist epistemology of conceptual analysis which he had developed. Condillac's emphasis on the logical manipulation of concepts based on commonplace wants permits the construction in *Le Commerce* of a system which strongly anticipates neoclassical theory.

In keeping with Condillac's stress on conceptual analysis *Le Commerce* opens with a call for language reform. 'Each science demands a particular language, because each has ideas of its own. It seems we must begin by making this language' (Condillac, 1947, volume 2, p.242). The Physiocrats are then rebuked for proceeding without having made such a language. Condillac consequently sets out to analyse the word *valeur* and to 'remove all those inexact ideas which are attached to it, and which often make the language of economics unintelligible' (Condillac, 1947, volume 2, p.248).

In keeping with subjectivism, and following Galiani, Condillac states that utility is the foundation of value. 'It is according to this utility that our estimation is higher or lower ... the value of something is thus founded on its utility' (Condillac, 1947, volume 2, p.245). This claim is buttressed by a rebuttal of a cost theory of value. 'A thing does not have value because it costs, as one supposes; but it costs because it has value'. Condillac illustrated his point by reference to the price of water at a place far from a river. When one pays the price for such water one pays the cost of water transport but only 'since I estimate that it is worth the expense of transport. ... It would be very surprising to pay for the expense of transport in order to obtain something one values at nothing' (Condillac, 1947, volume 2, p.246).[9]

Condillac used his utility theory to explain the origin of trade, and to establish the mutual gains from trade:

> What then do we owe to merchants? If, as is generally supposed, a product of equal value is always exchanged for another product of equal value,... there will always be the same amount of value or wealth. But it is untrue that in exchange one gives equal value for equal value. On the contrary, each of the contracting parties always gives a lesser for a greater. Indeed, if one always exchanged equal values, there would be no gain for any trader. (Condillac, 1947, volume 2. p.255)

Here Condillac made an important contribution to the notion that the market economy is a structure of mutual interdependence. He has identified why the market economy has this structure: it is because trade is mutually benefiting.

Condillac's stress on the mutual gains from trade puts the reader in mind of the neoclassical model of the pure exchange economy. There was potential here for producing something with a still greater resemblance to neoclassical economics, if Condillac had deployed the concept of maximizing man. This potential seems even greater given that Condillac had an extensive philosophical correspondence with Gabriel Cramer, who had provided utility maximization as a principle to solve the St Petersburg Paradox (Condillac, 1953). However, any hypothesis of instrumental maximization must surely have been discouraged by Condillac's early allegiance to Locke's views on that topic. In the *Essai sur l'Origine des Connaissances Humaines*, published 30 years before *Le Commerce*, Condillac denied instrumental rationality with a thoroughly Lockean vehemence: 'What prejudices, what blindness even in the person of the best understanding! Though their miscarriage shews them their error, yet they will not alter their conduct' (Condillac, 1971, p.86).[10] So while Locke's rationalist element fostered Condillac's rationalist epistemology, Locke's highly anti-rationalist psychology discouraged the notion of instrumental rationality, which would have complemented Condillac's theorizing so well. Nevertheless in *Le Commerce* instrumental rationality seems to play a definite, if unobtrusive role: for example, traders trade only because it improves their situation.

The notion of instrumental rationality may have been given some encouragement in the period between Condillac's earliest and last works by the writings of Claude-Adrien Helvétius (1715-71). In 1758 Helvétius had won notoriety with *De l'Esprit*, a 'parody' of Condillac's sensualism (Cassirer, 1951, p.25), which achieved a 'sweeping success' (Schumpeter, 1954, p.130). Helvétius's next work, *De l'Homme* of 1772, argued that self-interest was the great 'original principle' of human action. 'What in fact does the theatre of this world present to us? Nothing but the various and perpetual movements of interest. The more we meditate on this principle, the more we perceive its extent and fecundity. It is an inexhaustible mine of subtle and powerful ideas' (Helvétius, 1969, volume 2, p.359).[11] The importance of Helvétius in fostering Bentham's maximizing notions, both political and individual, is well known and well documented (Halévy, 1928, pp.19-21). Is it possible that Helvétius's strong positions also influenced Condillac?[12]

Helvétius is in addition an illustration of how meaningless an avowal of empiricist principles had become by about 1770. In epistemology Helvétius presents himself as a strict empiricist. 'Philosophy cannot advance without the staff of experience: it does indeed advance but constantly from observation to observation, *and where observation is wanting it stops*' (Helvétius, 1969, volume 1, p.99). In reality, Helvétius is an extreme rationalist. His writings are doctrinaire and deductivist. He claims to be able to offer 'geometrical proofs' and the 'most rigorous demonstration' of his contentions. At another point he says: 'it is on the knowledge of a first fact, from which all those of nature may be deduced, that the discovery of the system of the world depends ...' (Helvétius, 1969, volume 1, p.211). With more self-knowledge, he observes, 'Far from condemning a systematic spirit, I admire it in great men. It is to the efforts made to destroy or defend those systems that we doubtless owe an infinity of discoveries' (Helvétius, 1969, volume 1, p.248).

6.4 Conclusion

Condillac and Turgot worked on a similar project to Hume, with similar materials. They all sought to further the Science of Man using the inheritance of the 17th century philosophers, and their developers in the early 18th century. All three gave a more rationalist treatment of economic questions than they had previously received. But Condillac and Turgot also exemplify the greater resistance of the French *philosophes* to anti-rationalism. These two authors gave 'hypothesis' and 'abstraction' far more due than they received from Hume and Montesquieu. Their outlook favoured economic theory, which they practised with proficiency. But this outlook was also vulnerable to empiricist criticism.

Notes

1 Condillac had known Turgot since meeting him in the salons of Paris during the 1740s.
2 'What renders general ideas so necessary, is the limited capacity of the human mind' (Condillac, 1971, p.139; see also Condillac, 1947, volume 1, p.739).
3 Theoretical medicine was another example of a philosophical system. Condillac was as censorious of theoretical medicine as John Locke: '... the doctors who follow the method that I reprove ... relate everything to general assumptions that they have adopted, ... with a general system there are barely any illnesses which they do not seem to penetrate to the causes and discover remedies from a first glance' (Condillac, 1947, volume 1, p.198).
4 This is a fallacy. We might contrast Turgot's fallacy with Mandeville's plain understanding that two different theories may fit the truth equally well.
5 The view that economic principles are analytic has been adapted by later writers, including Hutchison (1938) and Harrod (1966). Harrod judged Keynesian and Marshallian economics to be barely anything more than a set of definitions. 'It is true to say that the Keynesian scheme consisted in essence in a set of new definitions and a re-classification. He asked us to look upon the multifarious phenomena of business life, and order them in our minds in a different way. In a certain sense one cannot dogmatically affirm one way to be right and the other to be wrong' (Harrod 1966, p.463). See also Harrod, 1966, p.143.

6 The closest parallel in Condillac to induction, the movement from particulars to generalization, is the movement from particulars to the abstract (that is, the process of abstraction). For example, in the *Essai sur l'Origine des Connaissances Humaines* Condillac writes '... we ought to have made a diligent study of particular truths, and to have ascended by different abstractions up to universal experience' (Condillac, 1971, p.74). Condillac gave abstraction the same role which Hume gave induction.

7 Schelle: 'It seems that in philosophy, Turgot had drawn a bit from everyone; one sees him now near to Descartes, next with Locke and Condillac. It is as Du Pont wrote, "The philosophy of Turgot was a thoughtful choice of what he found reasonable in all philosophers"' (Schelle in Turgot, 1913, volume 1, p.64).

8 Streissler has detailed the importance of Condillac in kindling the subjectivist analysis of value which was predominant in the older German Historical School. 'Menger evidently learnt from Roscher the importance of Condillac for his own subjectivism' (Streissler, 1990, p.47). Klein supplies some detail on the possible role of Condillac in fostering the subjectivist theories of value in France (Klein, 1985). Groenewegen (1983) has suggested Turgot's writings may have encouraged Bailey's subjectivism.

9 Schumpeter (1954a, p.1054) faults Condillac for explaining the utility of water by reference to the effort of drinking it. This is a misreading. The effort of drinking is a proof of the utility of water, not the source of its utility.

10 Further to the same point, Condillac's *Dissertation sur la Liberté* of 1754 is a standard Lockean treatment of human decision making.

11 In sympathy with his rationalist epistemology, Helvétius adopted the rationalist postulate that all men have the same natural mental powers. He writes '... every man who will, may understand all truths in the sublime science of geometry and the depths of fluxions, provided they be properly explained' (Helvétius, 1969, volume 1, p.230).

12 Smith owned copies of *De l'Esprit* and *De l'Homme* (Mizuta, 1967). But Oncken (1897) effectively disposes of the notion that Smith's introduction in 1767 to Helvétius, and the company of Nos 16-18 rue Saint-Anne, shifted him from a position of sympathy in the *Theory of Moral Sentiments* to a position of egoism in the *Wealth of Nations*.

7. Condillac, Turgot and the 'Classic Spirit'

The last chapter analysed the 'contribution' of Condillac and Turgot as consisting of the assimilation of Lockeanism into an older rationalistic outlook, and the application of the resulting false empiricism to economics. They thereby added impetus to the theoretical drift of economic thought which had begun with Hume and Montesquieu.

This chapter turns from interpretation to evaluation. It examines two critical reactions to the method of Condillac and Turgot: that of David Hume and that of Hippolyte Taine (1828-1893). Both critics objected to the overly theoretical bent of these thinkers; both believed that the method of Condillac and Turgot wrongfully neglected the variability of reality. But Taine's objection was deeper than Hume's. Taine's objection was metaphysical in nature, unlike Hume's. To Hume Turgot's abstract method was not fundamentally at fault; it was merely an over-ardent application of the proper search for the 'common and critical' circumstance. But to Taine the abstractionists' search for common and general truth was in itself misguided; explanatory power often lies in what is different, rather than what is common. Therefore to Taine the method of Condillac and Turgot must fail. Taine's outlook is not far from that of Montesquieu, so we might see Taine as standing in for Montesquieu. The difference between Taine's and Hume's criticisms reflects the differences between Hume and Montesquieu which we touched on in Chapter 5.

Hume also objected to one metaphysical aspect of Turgot's work: he rejected Turgot's doctrine that historical change was characterized by progress. The close of the chapter reviews that difference of opinion.

7.1 Taine's critique of the classic spirit

In *Les Origines de la France Contemporaine* (1876), Taine advanced a critique of a certain 'classic spirit' which, he believed, 'held sway over almost all French thinking from the close of the 17th century to the opening of the 19th.' This 'classic spirit' was no other than the 'rationalism' which this study has been concerned with. In epistemological terms, the classic spirit was a frame of mind in which the faculty of observation atrophied, and the faculty of reason burgeoned. This atrophied capacity for observation resulted in a blindness to existing variation, an incapacity to notice the individual, the singular, the special, the different. To quote Taine, there was among the *philosophes* of the 18th century an obliviousness to the 'characteristic detail, the animating fact, the specific circumstance....' (1876, p.202). Consequently, the spirit was 'powerless to fully portray or to record the infinite and varied details of experience' (1876, p.191). The mental storehouse of the spirit, he complains, found room only 'for a portion of the truth, a scanty portion' (1876, p.192).

Correlated with their inability to absorb details, the *philosophes* were preoccupied with generalities. As a low-resolution photograph can only detect the most general features of a topography, so the classic spirit absorbed only the most general features of human existence. This preoccupation with generalities impoverished their appreciation of human nature.

> In the eighteenth century the portrayal of living realities of an actual individual, just as he is in nature and in history, that is to say, ... a complete organism of peculiarities and traits, ... is improper. The capacity to receive and contain all these is wanting. Whatever can be discarded is cast aside, and to such an extent that nothing is left at last but a condensed extract, an evaporated residuum, an almost empty name, in short, what is called a hollow abstraction.' (1876, p.197)

Taine uses the paucity of characterization in classic drama as an illustration of how the spirit's limited capacity to receive dilutes the understanding of human nature.

> Its creations are not veritable individuals, but generalised characters, a king, a queen, a young prince [1876, p.195]...The character lacks the personal badge, the unique, authentic appellation serving as the primary stamp of an individual. [1876, p.197]...As to the circumstances of time and place, which exercise the most powerful influence in fashioning and diversifying man, it scarcely indicates them, making an abstraction of them. (1876, p.195)

Certain members of the Enlightenment were sensible to Taine's criticism of their age's penchant for colourless art. Adam Smith notes the thinness of characterization of that highly popular Enlightenment literary creation, Ossian. 'What perfect uniformity of Character do we find in *all the heroes described by Ossian*? And what variety of manners on the contrary, in those who are celebrated by Homer?' (quoted in Scott, 1937, p.342). The poetry of Ossian was further diluted in French translation. One of these diluters was Turgot, the first French translator of Ossian, whose efforts were characterized by 'a tendency always to moderate passion, to soften violence and jagged contours, to lose what is most wild and unconstrained in Macpherson's work' (Barratt, 1973, p.127).[1] The artistic forays of Smith and Turgot are more than just curious expressions of the classic spirit, since art in the 18th century was more than just an expression of the spirit: it was a powerful disseminating agent of it. Classic aesthetics, by advocating dogmatically the values of simplicity and generality, helped insinuate these criteria of judgement into scientific studies.

Taine held that the insinuation of these values of simplicity and generality into science had a scientific cost. To Taine, what was generally true was generally insignificant. Therefore, the classic spirit, in Taine's view, had a bias towards absorbing 'slight, unsubstantial *commonplaces* for its materials' (1876, p.192). By being blind to variation the spirit is blind to the fundamentals. Taine's charge therefore becomes one of superficiality. Taine complained that on reading the *philosophes*:

> it seems, ... that the climates, institutions and civilization which completely transform the human mind, are for it merely so many externals or accidental envelopes, which, far from reaching down to the depths, scarcely go below the surface. The prodigious difference which separates the men of two centuries, or of two races, escapes them entirely [1876, p.199].... In this vast moral and social world, they only remove the superficial bark from the human tree with its innumerable roots and branches; they are unable to penetrate to or grasp at anything beyond it; their hands cannot contain more. (1876, p.201)

Thus the error of the classic spirit is not merely to overgeneralize; it is to mistake externals for fundamentals; to mistake the easily apparent for the essential.

Can the two principal economic works of Condillac and Turgot be seen as part of the 'classic spirit'? Turgot's *Réflexions* is an entirely 'classic' work: it is a long, flat, featureless plain of generalization. The *Réflexions* contains not a single date, only two quantitative facts (the relative price of gold in China, and relative price of slaves in Guinea), a few remarks on the history of money, and the legal organisation of land cultivation in France.

In the classic (or rationalist) manner, Turgot found more significance in the unity of the world than in its diversity. He wrote of 'human kind always the same in its upheaval, as sea water in storms, ...'(Turgot, 1913, volume 1, p.56). Montesquieu's cultural relativism disgusted him. He castigated the 'stupidity' of the *Esprit des Lois* for throwing doubt on the existence of a unique natural order (Turgot, 1913, volume 3, p.477).[2] He rejected the notion that the 'custom of the country' should influence policy on the grounds that the 'unique natural order' should be respected.

Condillac's *Commerce* is also classic in tone. Condillac, like Turgot, believed the 'general character' of humankind 'is the same everywhere' (Condillac, 1947, volume 2, p.11). Condillac deploys this assumption in his extensive conjectures of world history. In sympathy with this assumption, Condillac's *Commerce* is composed entirely of very broad statements and is largely devoid of specific factual information. Condillac repeats a number of Cantillon's quantitative assertions, including one regarding the amount of food supplied to 'savages' by land. But even that is classical: 'savages' are just 'savages'; land is just 'land'; food is just 'food'. He reports the relative price of gold, silver and copper, but Condillac's chapter on money is very thin compared to, for example, Smith's in the *Wealth of Nations*. In Smith's chapter we learn of the commodity monies of Abyssinia, India, Newfoundland, Virginia, the West Indies, the 'antient Spartans' and the 'antient Romans', as well as receiving an explanation of Roman, English, Troyes and Scotch Pounds.

By restricting himself to general propositions Condillac conceded that he must sometimes make errors; but he says that does not matter: 'it matters little that some of these assumptions do not seem plausible' (Condillac, 1947, volume 2, p.322). One must tolerate the erroneousness of abstract propositions if one is to secure the simplicity, which in the true 'classic' manner, he was always seeking: 'I seek above all to simplify'; 'I want to simplify'; 'In order to simplify' (Condillac, 1947, volume 2, p.269). After all 'certainly, the truth is simple' (1947, volume 1, p.200).

By restricting himself to abstract or general propositions, Condillac also limited himself to truths which he grants to be mere commonplaces. He begins *Le Commerce* by avowing that he will spend much of his time on them. 'I will often speak of things very common. But if it is necessary to notice them in order to speak of other things with more precision, I will not be ashamed to say them' (Condillac, 1947, volume 2, p.242). The basis of his system is, he grants, propositions which 'appear to be trivial truths'.

With his slender base of bland, general propositions, Condillac obtains his results through demonstration. He adopts certain assumptions: 'Here are the assumptions', and then proves other propositions: 'We have proved' (Condillac, 1947, volume 2, p.362); 'in proving' (Condillac, 1947, volume 2, p.325); 'we have demonstrated' (Condillac, 1947, volume 2, p.366). It is true that Condillac did promise, in the preface to *Le Commerce*, to supply a third part which would consider economics 'with regard to the facts, in order to support myself by experience as much as by reasoning' (Condillac, 1947, volume 2, p.242). But this third part never appeared, and perhaps (probably?) was never written.

The work of Turgot and Condillac thus deserves the description of 'classic'.

But the generalizing propensity of Turgot and Condillac may not deserve the censure which Taine thought it warranted: Pareto, for one, defended the generalizing aspect of the *philosophes*. All science must abstract. Therefore, Pareto averred, the so-called classic spirit is just the theoretical spirit (Pareto, 1935, p.1245); it is the frame of mind which seeks to understand the world by devising and analysing models which capture the crucial aspects of reality, and discard the incidental.

Clearly a high degree of abstraction is not necessarily a ground for reproof. One should distinguish between successful, doubtful and unsuccessful abstraction. To impute relevance to irrelevance is a case of unsuccessful abstraction: the important bits have been dropped and only the 'husk' retained. But to identify the common and critical element, and to discard the irrelevant, is a piece of successful abstraction. Finally, to impute irrelevance to a relevant factor is a case of doubtful abstraction. It may yield an excellent approximation, or it may yield gross errors. Whether it makes for excellent accuracy or blatant error will be matter of debate, and one instance of doubtful abstraction was a matter of debate between Turgot and Hume.

7.2 Hume and Turgot on abstraction

Hume did not oppose abstraction in principle. In his own social analysis he sought to eliminate the 'superfluous circumstance'. He maintained, for example, that one can successfully ignore time and place in considering human nature. But Hume appears to have held that Turgot over-abstracted, and ignored important realities in his theorizing. The difference between Hume and Turgot manifested itself in their dispute of 1766 and 1767, over whether all taxes on consumption were passed on from workers to landowners by way of higher wages. Turgot believed they were. Hume retorted, 'You suppose then that the Labourers always raise the Price of their Labour in proportion to the Taxes. But this is contrary to Experience. There are almost no taxes on the English Colonies; yet Labour is three times dearer there than in any Country of Europe' (Hume, 1969, volume 2, p.94).

Turgot defended his claim on the basis of a distinction between the *current* and *fundamental* price of labour. The fundamental price will always include a full allowance for taxes. However, temporary shocks will push the current (or actual) price away from the fundamental price. With time the current price of labour will adjust to equal the fundamental price. 'I know that this action will not be sudden, and that in all complicated machines there are frictions which slow down the operations, no matter how infallibly they are demonstrated in theory' (Turgot, 1992, p.18). Turgot is claiming that his hypothesis that wages rise in proportion with taxes would work perfectly under 'ideal conditions', that is, conditions in which certain (supposedly) insignificant influences are absent.

Hume would be sympathetic to a method which claimed that fundamental forces are sometimes suppressed in the short run by insignificant factors; it is similar to his preference for reasoning about the general course of things to the neglect of the particular course of things. Yet there are differences between the two methods. Turgot was concerned with ideal entities, while Hume's reasoning about the general course of things is concerned with tendencies. Unlike ideal entities, the tendencies which interest Hume do not exclude disturbing events; disturbing events are part of the sum total of reality, from which the tendency is composed. Further, Hume denied the success of

Turgot's particular application of his method. Hume denied that taxes, even in the long run, affected wages as Turgot supposed. And in this denial was not Hume vindicated? The notion of an 'iron law of wages' was a dead end. By insisting on rigidly fixed after-tax real wages, Turgot was committing a type of error which all theoreticians are liable to: to miss the real uniformity, to impose a false uniformity on real variety, and then to dismiss the variety as merely 'frictions' which have no systematic explanatory role. Schumpeter called this error the 'Ricardian vice': the oversimplifications; the exogenizations; the under-admitting of the variety which the world teaches, to the neglect of the true fundamentals. Turgot was practising the Ricardian vice.[3]

Turgot's practice of the vice was encouraged by several things. It was facilitated by the methodology where errors are ascribed to departures from ideal conditions, rather than allow the possibility that even under ideal conditions the doctrine would be wrong.

The vice was also encouraged by Turgot's desire for simple policy decisions. For example, Turgot did not deny Quesnay's 'profound' analysis of circulation and reproduction, but recommended to Du Pont that reliance be placed instead on the principle of competition. This principle was 'more clear cut by its simplicity and by its generality without exception' (Turgot, 1913, volume 2, p.507), and, in any case, it provided by itself all the policy results of Quesnay's theory. In a similar vein, Turgot scorns Helvétius's claim that humankind is utility maximizing on the grounds that this claim has no 'practical results, since it is equivalent to saying *mankind wants only what he wants*' (Turgot, 1913, volume 2, p.638). But, in retrospect, a utility-maximizing approach would have served far better the general reasoning favoured by Turgot: it would have admitted some of the variability of the world, but at the same time traced it to a general principle, the principle of utility maximization. Until utility-maximizing choice was analysed the general reasoners of economics had little choice but to advance 'laws' which were defenceless against empiricist criticism.

Finally, the vice was also prompted by Turgot's feeling that arguing from facts would be inconclusive. Facts, Turgot complained, are easily contradicted (Turgot, 1913, volume 1, p.383). Disputes can only be resolved through theory. Again we see a contrast with Locke: whereas Locke despaired at the inconclusiveness of disputation by way of maxims and general principles, Turgot (like Quesnay) despaired at the inconclusiveness of disputation by way of facts. The possibility that it was rational for disputes to be inconclusive, given the facts at hand, did not seem to occur to him.

But Turgot's errors with the vice can only be known with hindsight. Neither Hume nor Turgot had any method for distinguishing 'vicious' from 'virtuous' abstraction. Neither does one exist today.

7.3 Progress and the 'usual returns of barbarism'

Hume also had a metaphysical disagreement with Turgot. Hume was equivocal about the notion that the world was a system with a beneficent purpose, and Turgot may have shared this equivocation. For although Turgot allowed a remote beneficent supervision by the Deity, his restless, reforming character surely indicates that he felt this supervision was not very rigorous. But if Turgot was ambivalent about the world as a beneficent system he did advocate a somewhat weaker doctrine with great force. In Turgot's mind historical change was characterized by progress: humankind always 'advanced towards its perfection'.

Turgot's doctrine of progress is a piece of metaphysical rationalism. It had been advocated by Leibniz, who had justified it through philosophic precepts. Turgot took up this piece of metaphysical rationalism, but gave it a firmly empiricist footing. Turgot justified his doctrine of progress thus: since our knowledge is increased by new experience, and since each passing year provides new experiences, each passing year leaves us with more knowledge. Turgot's 'trial and error' theory of progress is epistemologically anti-rationalist in that it rejects reasoning as the source of progress; it rejects the notion that human beings are equipped with a logic of discovery. It relies instead on human beings having a power to draw lessons from the chaotic flux in human affairs. 'There is no change [*mutation*] which occurs which does not lead to some advantage; for none is made without producing experience ...'(Turgot, 1913, volume 1, p.285).

Turgot's theory builds on the epistemological stances of earlier anti-rationalists, who themselves took steps towards a theory of progress. Dubos had earlier argued that the increase of knowledge required the accumulation of experience, and therefore the passage of time.[4]

Mandeville had taken up this notion in Note P of the *Fable of the Bees* and put it in a more optimistic light. Since knowledge increases with experience, and since experience increases with time, technical knowledge increases with the passage of time, and 'the very Poor lived richer than the Rich before'. Turgot's theory was essentially the same, but he did not limit the theory to technological and economic matters; he also applied it to political and social arrangements. In 1750 the youthful Turgot suggested that rather than hope for a legislative or administrative genius, political progress will occur without design in a trial and error fashion:

> Unhappy are those countries whose law makers have been led by a spirit of system ... Happier are those nations whose laws have not been established by genius; they are least perfect themselves, although slowly, and with a thousand detours, without principles, without designs, without a fixed project; chance and circumstances have often led to wiser laws than the search and effort of the human mind ....(Turgot, 1913, volume 1, p.208)[5]

Hume, however, was an adversary of the notion of progress. In June 1768 he wrote to Turgot:

> I know you are one of those, who entertain the agreeable and laudable, if not too sanguine hope, that human society is capable of perpetual Progress towards Perfection, that the Encrease of Knowledge will still prove favourable to good Government, and that since the Discovery of Printing we need no longer Dread the usual Returns of Barbarism and Ignorance. Pray, do not the late Events in this country appear a little contrary to your System? (Hume, 1969, volume 2, p.180[6])

To Hume the weak point in Turgot's theory of progress by trial and error was that it assumed that society *will* learn from its experience simply because it *can* learn from experience. But before one may conclude that society will learn simply because it has the opportunity to do so, one must ascertain the value this society places on new knowledge.[7] So, Hume was drawn to ask, what value does humankind place on knowledge? Humankind is not 'philosophic'; it is not naturally curious. It needed incentives before it would value knowledge. One incentive, certainly, was the material advantage derived from knowledge. Hume allowed trial and error improvement in matters of technology. Ship design was his example of how trial and error could yield with time what brilliant analysis could yield more quickly (Hume, 1987, p.513).[8]

Another incentive to knowledge was the pleasure of excelling over others. This clearly required the existence of others attempting to do the same thing, in other words, competition. Competitive situations also increased the material advantages to knowledge (and the costs of ignorance). In accordance with these considerations, Hume, Smith and Condillac believed progress would be promoted by competition. Hume related the progress of the arts and sciences in Ancient Greece to the competition between Greek city states.[9] Smith attributed the development of the English legal system to the competition between various courts (Smith, 1937, V, i, p.679). And Condillac explains the lack of progress in Egypt to monopolization of trades by hereditary guilds (Condillac, 1947, volume 2, p.40).

But there are still two more assumptions in Turgot's trial and error vision of progress which are vulnerable to anti-rationalist criticism. First, Turgot's vision neglects the possibility that the new situations which each passing year provide actually make the lessons from older experience obsolete. This would be plausible if, as Montesquieu supposed, human society were heterogeneous rather than uniform. In a world where new situations indicate a fundamental break with the past it is doubtful that the accumulation of experience will be instructive. Induction will not pay off, since the present does not resemble the past. Little wonder that Montesquieu paid little attention to progress, but considerable attention to genius, which Turgot scorned.[10]

Second, even if new experience is informative, and even if society wants to learn, trial and error progress assumes that society is sufficiently rational to learn from its trials and errors. This implicit assumption also makes progress vulnerable to anti-rationalist doubts about human intelligence.

However, not all theories of progress require rational learning. An alternative to trial by error progress, or evolution by learning, is evolution by 'survival of the fittest', or 'natural selection'. We might think those of a less rationalistic outlook would be drawn to such a theory of progress. In fact, Hume provides one of the earliest known hints at natural selection in a biological context.[11] In the *Dialogues Concerning Natural Religion*, written by 1751, Philo remarks: 'It is in vain, therefore, to insist upon the uses of the parts in animals or vegetables, and their curious adjustment to one another. I would fain know how could an animal subsist unless its parts were so adjusted? Do we not find that it immediately perishes whenever this adjustment ceases?' (Hume, 1948, p.54).

Historians of evolution have noted the traces of the stimulus which Hume's writings gave to later biological evolutionists, including Erasmus Darwin and Charles Darwin (Harrison, 1971, p.254). It has been pointed out, for example, that Charles Darwin records reading Hume's *Dialogues Concerning Natural Religion* and (apparently) other works of Hume between August 1838 and January 1839, the period of genesis of Darwin's theory, at least by his own account (Huntley, 1972, pp.458, 467).

However, doctrines of biological evolution by natural selection were rarely pressed with any determination in the 18th century (see Bremner, 1983). Perhaps this was because the very fact of biological evolution (by natural selection or otherwise) was little appreciated. Certainly, the proponents of cultural evolution were oblivious to it. Mandeville actually sought to contrast the presence of cultural evolution with the absence of biological evolution:

> Our Knowledge is advanced by slow Degrees, and some Arts and Sciences require the Experience of many Ages, before they have been brought to any tolerable Perfection. Have we any reason to imagine, that the Society of Bees, that sent forth the first Swarm, made worse Wax or Honey than any of their Posterity have produced since? And again, the laws of Nature are fix'd and unalterable ... (Mandeville, 1924, volume 2, p.187)

Turgot, too, contrasted the momentum of cultural evolution with the supposedly static character of nature that was 'enclosed in a circle of revolutions always the same' (Turgot, 1913, volume 1, p.215). And Hume, after floating the idea of natural selection in the *Dialogues*, claims that the actual extinction of any species on Earth is unknown.[12]

If the advocates of cultural evolution are completely unaware of the biological evolution by natural selection, the great exemplar of unplanned development, we might be less surprised that the idea of cultural development through the struggle between cultural forms seems not to be found anywhere in Hume, Mandeville or Smith. The notion of cultural evolution by a struggle for survival would also have been discouraged by the notions of the harmony of interests, and social balance, which the 18th century favoured.

Ironically, one of the rare hints at cultural development by selection in the 18th century was provided in an attempt to rebut the Hobbesian vision of social disharmony. Montesquieu, by way of rebutting Hobbes, presents in Letter 11 of the *Lettres Persanes* a tale of the Troglodytes. This tells of two societies: one without any social virtues, and another with all the social virtues. The virtuous society flourishes, and the vicious one perishes. Is this an attempt to teach the 'survival of the fittest' in cultural terms, or just a parable on the rewards to goodness, and the penalties to barbarity? In any case this hint at undesigned selection finds little articulation in the noticeably timeless approach to social structures of the *Esprit des Lois*.

7.4 Conclusion

Condillac and Turgot used an abstract method to provide some of the strongest 'anticipations' of the style of 19th century classical economics. This chapter has reviewed some 18th and 19th century criticisms of their method. Hume sympathized with their search for general and simple models, but disagreed with the strength of their abstractions. 'Relativist' critics of Condillac and Turgot, such as Taine, argued that their method of abstraction must fail, since the significant lay in the different rather than the common, and abstraction, therefore, unwittingly selected the irrelevant and discarded the essential.

The positions of Hume and relativists, such as Taine or Montesquieu, also made for critiques of Turgot's notion of progress. Montesquieu's vision of many heterogeneous forms of society meant that the knowledge content of past experience depreciated rapidly as society assumed different forms. Hume was less concerned about the obsolescence of past experience, but more concerned whether the knowledge content of past experience would ever be valued.

Notes

1 Barratt faults Turgot for using *pensif* to translate 'musing', *ouragan* to translate 'whirlwind', and *brise* for 'breeze'. Turgot admits of his translations, 'I do not flatter myself that I have conserved as well as the English translator [i.e. Macpherson] the

character of the original; our language, less rich, less simple and less bold, lends itself only with great difficulty to extraordinary phrases' (Turgot, 1913, volume 1, p.624).

2 Turgot's scorn for the *Esprit des Lois* was shared by Condorcet and Helvétius. But not by Hume. Hume says the *Esprit* has 'considerable merit' despite 'false refinement' and 'crude positions' (Hume, 1969, p.133).

3 It is curious to observe Malthus in 1817 rebutting Ricardo over the same point that Hume did Turgot. Malthus writes: 'A writer may, to be sure, make any hypothesis he pleases; but if he supposes what is not at all true practically, he precludes himself from drawing any practical inferences from his hypothesis. In your essay on profits you suppose the real wages of labour constant; but as they vary with every alteration in prices of commodities, (while they remain nominally the same) and are in reality as variable as profits, there is no chance of your inferences being just as applied to the actual state of things' (Ricardo, 1952, volume 7, p.122).

4 Turgot believed that Dubos was inclined 'to build systems on common prejudices and support them by the most strange paradoxes' (Turgot, 1913, volume 1, p.140). But Turgot attributes the discovery of the telescope to the play of a child, a story of Dubos (Turgot, 1913, volume 1, p.138).

5 It is little wonder that Du Pont excised this paragraph from his edition of Turgot's works.

6 Hume allowed that things 'ornamental to human life' advance 'towards perfection' (Hume, 1987, p.566).

7 One can put Hume's difference with Turgot another way. Hume agreed that a long passage of time was necessary for the growth of knowledge; he considers two thousand years 'a small space of time to give any tolerable perfection to the sciences' (Hume, 1911, volume 1, p.257). But he denied that a long passage of time was sufficient for the growth of knowledge.

8 'If we survey a ship, what an exalted idea must we form of the ingenuity of the carpenter who framed so complicated, useful, and beautiful a machine? And what surprise must we feel when we find him a stupid mechanic who imitated others, and copied an art which, through a long succession of ages, after multiplied trials, mistakes, corrections, deliberations, and controversies had been gradually improving?' Philo in Hume, 1948, p.39.

9 Notice the contrast here between Hume and Descartes. Hume attributed Greek progress to competition and political liberty. Descartes attributed it to the possession of the 'right method'; he suspected the Greeks had secretly employed such a method to acquire their geometry (Descartes, 1985, p.18).

10 Contrast Montesquieu's admiration of Lycurgus's 'breadth of genius' (Montesquieu, 1989, p.36), with Turgot's denigration of him (Turgot, 1913, volume 1, p.207).

11 Another early mention of the natural selection hypothesis is by Maupertuis in his *Essai de Cosmologie* of 1751 (Maupertuis, 1965, volume 1, p.11). See Lovejoy, 1909, p.243.

12 In Part XI of the *Dialogues* Philo observes, 'So well adjusted are the organs and capacities of all animals, and so well fitted to their preservation, that, as far as history or tradition reaches, there appears not to be any single species which has yet been extinguished in the universe' (Hume, 1948, p.75).

8. Physiocracy and the first crisis of abstraction

The advent of Physiocracy seems to disrupt the scene traced in earlier chapters. We have argued that Hume, Condillac and Turgot sought to integrate, with greater or lesser success, the rationalist and anti-rationalist sentiments of the 17th century. But Physiocracy seems unconcerned with this project. It often contented itself with an extravagant methodology of *a priori* certainty. It was convinced of the necessary existence of a 'natural order', and awaited a legislator of sufficient genius to implement it. Perplexing the critic still further is the appearance that Quesnay (their Master, Confucius and John the Baptist), did not always share all the exalted methodological pretensions of his disciples. In this chapter it is suggested that Quesnay was actually part of the project of integration, however disjointed his own efforts may have been.

The excesses of Physiocracy brought a reaction at the close of the 1760s, in what was the first methodological controversy in economics. This reaction has sometimes been interpreted as empiricist in inspiration. It was, however, only in part an empiricist censure of the *a priori* method of Physiocracy. The most prominent critic of Physiocracy, Ferdinando Galiani, was not an empiricist. His method was explicitly *a priori*. The basis of Galiani's objection to Physiocracy was not epistemological; it was metaphysical: to Galiani truth was always time- and place-specific, and never universal. Galiani, then, represents a protest of the relativism of Montesquieu against the absolutism of Physiocracy.

8.1 Quesnay's philosophizing

How can one begin to understand François Quesnay (1694-1774)? His 'Tableau' still stands uncomprehended. His method is almost equally difficult to grasp. He appears to have adopted inconsistently empirical and rationalist methods. Fox-Genovese has observed that Quesnay has been 'variously identified as a rationalist and an empiricist, as a Cartesian and a Lockean. His thought has been linked to that of Plato, the Schoolmen, Shaftesbury, Cumberland, Descartes, Leibniz and Wolff' (Fox-Genovese, 1976, p.77). Whereas to Schumpeter Quesnay 'made an analysis of facts the main point' (Schumpeter, 1954b, p.48), to Foley Quesnay's 'contribution' was merely to obliterate the empirical element in Cantillon (Foley, 1973, p.40).

What is certain is that Quesnay's first philosophical loyalty was rationalist. As a young man he had a relish for Malebranche's *Recherche* (Kubota, 1958). Malebranche remained in Quesnay's mind a 'great man', 'this wise philosopher, this philosopher so logical in his reasonings' (quoted in Kubota, 1958, p.186). In the *Essai Physique sur l'Économie Animale* Quesnay compares Malebranche very favourably to John Locke. He expresses surprise that 'after the profound researches that Malebranche has made on the nature of our ideas, Locke has been so diffuse and obscure on a subject that has been treated so skilfully' (Quesnay, 1888, p.745). Locke ignored the 'intellectual faculty' in our minds, and confused it with sensation. 'After a tedious reading one sees that the author [John Locke] has only obscure, imperfect, very vague and very confused ideas of human understanding' (Quesnay, 1888, p.745).[1]

Quesnay's sole strictly philosophic work, his article of 1756 on 'Evidence' in the *Encyclopédie*, is a manifestation of this influence of Malebranche. 'Evidence' is a term highly charged with rationalist suggestion, since it is only from 'evident' principles that any inquiry could proceed. What is evidence to Quesnay? Quesnay explains: 'I mean by evidence a certainty which is as impossible for us to deny as it is to ignore our actual sensations' (Quesnay, 1958, volume 2, p.398).

Recall Malebranche's test of evidence:

> *We must give full consent only to those propositions that appear so evidently true that we cannot withhold our consent without feeling inner pain and the secret reproaches* of reason, *i.e. without our knowing clearly that we would make ill use of our freedom were we to withhold our consent.* (Malebranche, 1980, p.409)

The definitions of Quesnay and Malebranche seem similar: 'cannot withhold our consent'; 'impossible for us to deny'. But the similarity is actually not so close. Malebranche uses the 'reproach of reason' as the test of evidence, while Quesnay uses the force of external sensations. The proper parallel to Quesnay's definition lies with John Locke, not Malebranche. In Chapter ii of Book IV of the *Essay Concerning Human Understanding,* Locke considers the notion of 'degrees of evidence'. He writes there of the 'clearest and most certain' knowledge we are capable of: an example is 'white is not black'. He continues, 'This part of knowledge is irresistible, and, like bright sunshine, forces itself immediately to be perceived, as soon as ever the mind turns its view that way ... *It is on this intuition that depends all the certainty and evidence of all our knowledge* ... ' (Locke, 1959, IV, ii, 1). It is Locke's sensualist (and externalist) criterion of evidence (rather than the internalist one of 'reproach' of Malebranche) which is the one adopted by Quesnay.

Indeed, Quesnay's article on 'Evidence' is in large part a confident profession of the empiricist doctrine of knowledge.[2] Quesnay, following Locke, rejects both axioms and innate ideas as a starting point for knowledge (Quesnay, 1958, volume 2, pp.399,409). Knowledge begins, says Quesnay, with sensation: 'the exercise of our senses is the principle of all certainty and the foundation of all our knowledge' (Quesnay, 1958, volume 2, p.406). The intellect is relegated to a secondary role in the acquisition of knowledge. Quesnay, following Condillac, reduces judging and arguing to sensation (Quesnay, 1958, volume 2, p.403).[3] Abstract ideas are only 'confused and imperfect recollections' of particular sensations (Quesnay, 1958, volume 2, p.411). Abstract ideas are no more than expedients 'to avoid a collection of particular ideas' which would be burdensome owing to the 'very limited capacity' of our minds. Even as expedients abstractions remain doubtful, since they 'continually lead astray' humankind (Quesnay, 1958, volume 2, p.411).

So in 'Evidence', rather than follow Malebranche, Quesnay seems to have inverted the whole rationalist outlook. To rationalists the ordinary senses were unreliable and easily tricked, but the 'mind's eye' would not be tricked as long as it applied itself to 'the evident'. To Quesnay the mind's eye is easily tricked, but the ordinary senses are reliable: they are what constitute evidence. What distinguishes Quesnay from Locke is not the empiricism of Locke, but the steely confidence of Quesnay's own empiricism. The pessimism of Locke about the possibility of knowledge is wholly absent in 'Evidence'. Quesnay announces there: 'There is a certain and constant

correspondence between bodies and the sensations they supply us ...
from whence results an evidence or a certainty of knowledge which
we cannot refuse' (Quesnay, 1958, volume 2, p.405). Quesnay seems
to have taken the optimism of rationalists about the possibility of
knowledge and joined it to the empiricist doctrine of the source of
knowledge.

However, Quesnay's strident avowal of empiricist principles in
'Evidence' sits uneasily with the methods he often actually used in his
economics. In *Le Despotisme de la Chine*, for example, Quesnay
extols the intellect, scorns historical inquiry and contents himself
unsubstantiated general claims.[4]

8.2 Quesnay le médecin

A better insight into Quesnay's methodology may be obtained from
his career in medicine. We have stressed how medicine had been a
continual battleground of rationalist and empiricist methods. We are
fortunate that Quesnay was interested in medical methodology and
twice wrote at length on the topic. These essays reveal a stance which
blends theory and empirics, frequently leaning towards theory,
sometimes towards experience.

In 1736 Quesnay published an *Essai Physique sur l'Économie
Animale* which contains a 56-page methodological preface devoted to
what he describes as the incessant 'war' between theory and
experience. Quesnay judged there to be merit and demerit in both
sides in the war and calls for a truce.

Quesnay began with the proposition that theory is 'indispensable'.
He rejects the empiricist tenet that medicine should seek cures from
experience, without troubling with theoretical foundations. If such an
atheoretical empiricism worked, he said, medicine would have
acquired successful law-like rules in treating illness by the time of his
own century. But in fact many empirically based treatments were
absurd and credulous, and medical progress largely consisted of
culling medicine of these absurdities. The reason why so many
empirically based treatments were absurd is that in the matter of cures
experience is 'almost always ambiguous, leaves us undecided and
sometimes even mistaken' (Quesnay, 1736, p.xiii). It is ambiguous
since inferences from experience were always based on the *post hoc*

ergo propter hoc fallacy; for example, the recovery followed the treatment, therefore the treatment caused the recovery. Mindful of this fallacy, Quesnay castigated the 'miserable empiricist', who 'justifies his bad practise by a great number of cures he thinks he has made'. He lamented how even the 'grandest men' have been left in illusion by such experience (Quesnay, 1736, p.xvii).

The fallacy of *post hoc ergo propter hoc* led Quesnay to urge doctors 'never to neglect theory', which he defines as that which explains and gives causes. These causes will come from anatomy, chemistry and physics. At that fundamental level experience will actually prove useful, since in the setting of the laboratory *post hoc ergo propter hoc* problems of inference are diminished. So it is by way of laboratory experiments, the kind which won Quesnay his medical reputation, that one will discover the principles of anatomy and chemistry (Quesnay, 1736, p.xxii); one will learn of those materials which 'harden' the humours, those which 'liquefy' them, those which 'thin' them, etc (Quesnay, 1736, p.xlvi). So although the advantages of experience are 'not very large when it is alone, but when it is seconded to a solid theory it is the base by which we can dare to advance little by little' (Quesnay, 1736, p.xx).

Quesnay came closest to summarizing his outlook when he recommended physicians to 'build a system, a system which, in truth, holds all the general experience of which we have spoken; but without which this experience would always appear discordant' (Quesnay, 1736, p.xxxvii). Quesnay evidently believed that this 'system' which reconciles and gives concord to the facts is a modified version of Galenic humoural theory.[5]

Quesnay advanced similar views on medical method in a *mémoire* of 1743 presented to the Académie Royale de Chirurgie (Quesnay, 1888, p.723). In this paper he presented himself as a moderate rationalist. He repeated his criticism of the empiricist's stress on observation of illness. He claimed the foolish 'prejudices' of the Ancients were 'founded on observations' since 'medicine and surgery were based almost exclusively on facts that had been noticed in practice ... [and] practitioners persisted all the more stubbornly in their disputes since they believed nature was speaking clearly in their favour ...' (Quesnay, 1888, p.725). 'Two thousand years have not been able to disabuse the most exact observers of these ridiculous dogmas

... so the sick have thus delivered their blood and life to the whim of doctors and surgeons on the strength of the most equivocal observations ...' (Quesnay, 1888, p.725). It was only after the arrival of 'experimental natural science' that 'anatomical researchers and physical discoveries have dissipated these errors ...' (Quesnay, 1888, p.726). Quesnay's emphasis on the existence of a 'right method' for making discoveries makes a clear contrast with anti-rationalists such as Dubos. His stress on 'experimental natural science' (i.e. physics and anatomy) makes a clear contrast with empirical physicians such as Sydenham and Mandeville. His fear that facts may only lengthen disputes has a counterpart in similar fears of Turgot.

Quesnay concluded that medicine is in need of an 'illuminating and deep theory'. What is this theory? 'Knowledge drawn from physical science, deduced from nature and the operation of remedies, combined with the causes of our illnesses, the observations of their symptoms, and the laws of animal economy, form the true theory without which there is neither art nor method on the treatment of disease' (Quesnay, 1888, p.734). As in 1736, Quesnay's goal remains explanation by way of fundamentals.

In keeping broadly with his mixed epistemological stance, Quesnay's own practice included elements of both empirical and theoretical reasonings. He adopted Daniel Bernoulli's mechanical theory of muscular action. On the other hand, he recommended the use of quinine, that favoured fever remedy of Locke and other empiricists, even though its use lacked a theoretical rationale. Even more characteristic of his methodological stance was his use of laboratory experiment: in his first medical publication he reported experiments on the flow of fluids, which supposedly constituted a test of doctrines of bleeding.

Quesnay's critics have divided over the relative importance of empirical and theoretical reasonings in his work. The majority have emphasized the 'theoretical' aspects. To Adam Smith Quesnay was a 'very speculative' physician (Smith, 1937, V, i, 3, p.638). Du Pont says that by his medical works Quesnay 'took his place amongst the leading metaphysicians, which was his most particular vocation' (Du Pont, 1984, p.237). A sympathetic contemporary medical critic judged in 1778 that Quesnay was often 'deaf to the voice of experience and observation in order to listen only to the words of his imagination'

(Eloy, 1973, p.9). Modern critics have deprecated Quesnay's medicine as laden with occult qualities: 'retentives, impulsives or irascibles ... Molière is not really far away' (Sutter, 1958, p.203).

On the other hand the medical historian Rousseau has classified Quesnay as an 'empirical doctor' (1972, p.157). These highly divergent judgements reflect the double-faced aspect of Quesnay's medicine, and form a parallel with the divergent judgements of his economic method.[6]

In the light of his use of both empirical and theoretical methods in medicine it is less surprising that Quesnay was not only the analyst of the zig-zag, but was also the student of empirical agronomy. In the light of the overall theoretical bias of his medical practise, it is less surprising that in his economics doctrinal pronouncements loom larger than his empirical efforts, in spite of his profession of an ardent empiricism in 'Evidence'.

8.3 The Master's disciples

In contrast to the Master, few of Quesnay's disciples troubled to do homage to empiricist precepts. Rather they provide the earliest examples in economics of confidence in a purely demonstrative method.

One of the more curious illustrations of the commitment to the *a priori* method by the Physiocrats is provided by Du Pont (Du Pont, 1955). In 1774 he submitted to Daniel Bernoulli an analysis of tax incidence. This used a geometrical method on the grounds that 'higher mathematics' is as applicable to political economy as it is to mechanics. Du Pont claimed that Bernoulli 'approved' of his memoir, and expressed the hope that Bernoulli would become the Huygens of political economy. What did the theorist of expected utility make of Du Pont's 'curves of price to sellers and buyers'?

The most perfect expression of dogmatic Physiocratic *a priorism* is found in Mercier de la Rivière's *L'Ordre Naturel et Essential des Sociétés Politiques* of 1767. The title page bears a quote from Malebranche: 'Order is the Law of Minds; and nothing is settled if it does not conform to it'. This was drawn from Malebranche's *Traité de Morale* where Malebranche had urged that the Prince be ruled by reason rather than by example (May, 1950), just the sort of thing the Physiocrats would wish to hear.

L'Ordre commences with the words 'It is evident ...', and the expression recurs every few pages. Mercier defines evidence in the manner of Malebranche, rather than Locke: 'An evident thing is a truth that a sufficient examination has yielded so perceptible, so manifest, that it is no longer possible for the human mind to imagine reasons to doubt it ...' (Mercier, 1910, p.46). The example given of such 'evident' truth are the truths of geometry. In Mercier's use of evidence we are an infinite distance from Quesnay's bidding his critics, in the *Dialogues sur le Commerce*, to 'Look about the farms and workshops and see'.

If the Master and the disciples differed to some extent over the source of knowledge, all seem equally convinced that this source provided certain knowledge, and that Physiocracy was a depository of certain knowledge. The historians of Physiocracy have collected many examples of the often quite preposterous, but wholly characteristic, superconfidence of the Physiocrats in their doctrine (Neill, 1949, pp.537-44; 1948, p.167). It was this extreme confidence that gave the peculiar, 'religious' aspect to their method, which defined them as a school, and which distinguished them from the rest of the thinkers we examine.

The Master and the disciples were also almost in concord in their conviction of the existence of a natural order, rooted in the physical world. This conviction was an enthusiastic manifestation of the craving for harmony which was seen earlier in Leibniz and Malebranche. This natural order differed from the social equilibrium of Montesquieu. It was absolute, rather than relative. It was a structure of hierarchy, rather than mutual interdependence. The Physiocrats reviled the balanced constitutions Montesquieu had pondered; authority must descend in a straight line from the rational despot. In economic matters, too, there was a structure of hierarchy. Physical laws are at the base of the hierarchy, 'productive' land at the next stage, and every economic activity rested on land; there was no mutual interdependence between the sectors of the economy. (This attitude is exemplified by Mercier's judgement that international trade is 'only a stop-gap and necessary evil', Mercier, 1910, p.262.) In their hierarchical vision of the structure of society and economy Physiocrats also exhibit a reversion to the 17th century rationalism of Descartes and Malebranche.

8.4 Diatribes and dialogues

The Physiocrats were soon subject to admonishment. One early expression of dissatisfaction was found in James Steuart's *Principles of Political Economy* of 1766. This book is seasoned with a certain amount of relativist sentiment.

> According to my way of treating this subject no *general* rules can be laid down in political matters: every thing *there* must be considered according to the circumstances and the spirit of the nations to which they relate. [Steuart, 1966, volume 1, p.4] .... I am not fond of condemning opinions; but I am very much for limiting general propositions. I have hardly ever escaped being led into error by every one I have laid down. (Steuart, 1966, volume 1, p.67)

Some critics have rightly detected in Steuart's outlook the mark of Montesquieu (Fletcher, 1937). But to be a relativist is not necessarily to be an empiricist, and other critics have stressed the amount of theoretical technique which Steuart allows himself: 'Steuart is one of the first writers to make an attempt to employ the scientific methods of isolation and abstraction in economic analysis. Long before Von Thünen we find him carrying on economic analysis on the basis of a closed economy' (Sen, 1957, p.28).

The methodological engagement between the Physiocrats and their critics, the first methodological debate in economics, began in earnest four years later in 1770, with the publication of Ferdinando Galiani's *Dialogues sur les Bleds* (see Venturi, 1972, chapter 8; Kaplan, 1976, volume 2, pp.590-613; Davison, 1985, chapter 6).

Ferdinando Galiani (1728-87) had already established himself as a value theorist by writing *Della Moneta* (1955), published in 1751. *Della Moneta* made a contrast with the writings of Mandeville, Hume, Montesquieu, Turgot and Condillac. All these last authors are empiricist in aspiration, if not in deed. The core of *Della Moneta* is straightforwardly *a priori*. After a first chapter devoted to a learned history of money, Galiani began his work proper with the complaint that earlier theories of value were not composed of 'clear and distinct' ideas (1955, p.48), and were consequently constructed on a false foundation. He then posited his own foundation and 'demonstrates' the 'exact' consequences. He concluded that the economic system is characterized by stability and a 'marvellous' equilibrium. He exultantly advances his own 'invisible hand' principle, by which the base passions of men are directed towards the good of all. This highly rationalist vision is combined with his own ardently advocated subjectivist theory of value. So Galiani, too, in *Della Moneta*, is part of the synthesis. Reason ruled everywhere, except, critically, in value, where passion was the unaccountable master. This synthesis is essentially the position of neoclassical economics.

After *Della Moneta* Galiani put aside political economy for 20 years. As a functionary in the Neapolitan embassy in Paris during the 1760s Galiani became a popular member of the salons. Some critics have identified him as favouring liberalizing economic policies in this period. This position would certainly fit in with *Della Moneta*, though in the judgement of others there is no hard evidence to support this identification (Kaplan, 1976, volume 2, p.593).

Somehow, and at some time, Galiani acquired a hatred of Physiocracy, and their programs of grain liberalization. By 1770 he had come to the opinion that the Physiocrats were 'a veritable occult sect, with all the faults of sects, jargon, system, a taste for persecution, a hatred for outsiders, snapping, spite and small mindedness' (Galiani, 1881, volume 1, p.114): 'They have prophecies, fables, visions and above all this, stupefying tediousness. If you want me to be frank, I think Quesnay is the Antichrist and his rural physiognomy is the Apocalypse' (Galiani, 1881, volume 1, p.129).

Galiani's animosity found a more measured expression in the *Dialogues sur le Commerce des Bleds*, which Galiani began composing in November 1768 (Davison, 1985, p.61). The final production was assisted by the editing of Diderot and Madame d'Épinay. Published in 1770, it was a great success. To Voltaire the *Dialogues* reached the same height as Plato and Molière. The Physiocrats were stung badly by its popularity, and arranged three rebuttals (including one by Mercier and one by Morellet). But what was all the fuss about? The historian of economic thought who seeks a substantive doctrinal contribution in the *Dialogues* will be wholly disappointed. The *Dialogues* make little contact with the fundamental questions of value and distribution, which surely underlie an analysis of the grain liberalization. However, the public was not seeking economic theory, but 'spirit', wit and riposte, which the *Dialogues* liberally supply. Galiani seemed to concede his own superficiality: 'It is devilishly profound because it is hollow, and there is nothing beneath it' (Galiani, 1881, volume 1, p.59).

Galiani's objections to grain liberalization were basically political. Liberalization would subvert the existing order, which is based on the exploitation of agriculture (Galiani, 1881, volume 1, p.329). His objections were, to a lesser degree, methodological. Galiani had by this time a horror of all general doctrines: 'general reasonings and nothing are pretty much the same thing. The economists think that with four big, vague words, and a dozen general reasonings, one knows everything, and I have proved they know nothing' (Galiani, 1881, volume 2, p.275).

Galiani's horror of general doctrines flows from the fact that he was, in metaphysical terms, an anti-rationalist. To the Galiani of 1770, the world was a heap, not an order. To the Galiani of 1770 the critical truth was that the world lacks uniformity and stability.[7] A slight shock will have major reverberations: an unusual purchase of five or six sacks of wheat will disturb the grain market of an entire province for a considerable time (Galiani, 1968, p.178). (Shades of the butterfly theorems of chaos theorists!) A small change in circumstances will substantially alter the optimal policy: 'in Political Economy a single change makes an immense difference: a canal dug, a port built, a province acquired ...' (Galiani, 1968, p.59). Whether a country is encircled by ocean, or is a huge 'limitless' country (Russia, North America) makes a substantial difference to proper policy.

In stressing the heterogeneity of human situations, Galiani is following a path marked earlier by Montesquieu. Galiani's prescription of differing economic policies for countries of differing geographical size is reminiscent of Montesquieu's dictum (in Book 8 of *Esprit des Lois*) that small countries should be republics, middling countries republics and large countries despotisms. Galiani's defence of the wisdom of ancient laws, his tendency to impute a material cause to the spirit of the people (Galiani, 1968, p.100), and his conservative instinct, are all reminiscent of Montesquieu. It is little wonder that Galiani speaks of Montesquieu as a 'great' man (Galiani, 1968, p.117) and the *Esprit des Lois* as 'the best book we have of its kind' (Galiani,

1968, p.117). Galiani's only criticism of Montesquieu is that he, too, over-generalized (Galiani, 1968, p.117). Galiani, therefore, represents an accentuation of the relativism of Montesquieu.

Galiani's relativism had two consequences. First, it necessitated his rejection of the absolute legitimacy of any system, including *laissez-faire*. He specifically rejected the notion, which he had held so gladly in 1751, that there is beneficent order; to Galiani of 1770 nature is hostile, not hospitable (Galiani, 1968, p.225).

Second, Galiani's relativism made successful empiricism impossible. Since the outcome of any policy is so critically sensitive to circumstance, one can only draw lessons about the present situation from other situations which are exactly the same (Galiani, 1968, pp.56,58). But circumstances never are the same, said Galiani, and so experience can never guide policy. For example, he explicitly rejected the notion that the experience of other societies can form a guide to French grain policy (Galiani, 1968, p.58). Galiani, then, is a definite anti-empiricist. His relativism pushed him towards an anti-inductivist epistemology, just as the relativism of Montesquieu encouraged an anti-inductivist epistemology. In typical rationalist fashion Galiani approached the world as a problem to be figured out by those with sufficient wits. His means for figuring out this problem was the deductive method, beginning with simple cases, and building up to more complex ones. This method he described himself as Euclidean (Galiani, 1968, pp.65,67,68). Galiani was as *a priori* in 1770 as he was in 1751.

It is clear, then, that critics who have supposed Galiani's hostility to general theories and Physiocracy arose from an empiricist inclination are mistaken (Venturi, 1972, pp.183,184). Galiani's dispute with the general theories of the Physiocrats was not epistemological, but metaphysical. Galiani was not sharply distinguished from the Physiocrats by any empiricism, even though it is tempting to suppose so, and Diderot himself did so.[8] Galiani's position can in fact be contrasted with that of the most significant advocate of long, 'daily experience', David Hume.

Hume shared Galiani's rage against the Physiocrats. In July 1769 he wrote to Morellet:

> I see that ... you take care not to disoblige your economists ... But I hope that in your work you will thunder them, and crush them, and pound them, and reduce

them to dust and ashes! They are, indeed, the set of men the most chimerical and most arrogant that now exist, since the annihilation of the Sorbonne. I ask your pardon for saying so, as I know you belong to that venerable body. (Hume, 1969, p.205)

Hume's fury is not difficult to understand; Physiocracy epitomized the notion of theory as a 'revealed religion', almost literally. Physiocracy was, in the judgement of one of its advocates, the 'policy of Heaven'. Even more temperate associates of the sect, including Morellet, were not shy of resting their case on the 'sacred' right of property.

But Hume's quarrel with the Physiocrats has a different origin to Galiani's. The heart of Hume's quarrel is epistemological, while Galiani's is metaphysical. Hume essentially agreed with the Physiocrats' presumption of general laws, but disagreed with how they obtained them: to Hume laws should be based on experience, not 'evidence'. (Thus Hume's disagreements with the Physiocrats is essentially the same as his disagreement with Turgot.) Galiani, in contrast, violently disagreed with the Physiocrats' presumption of general laws, but essentially concurred with their *a priori* method. So Hume was metaphysically rationalist and epistemologically anti-rationalist, while Galiani was metaphysically anti-rationalist and epistemologically rationalist.

The difference between Hume and Galiani is reflected in the differences in their approaches to devising policy. Galiani's approach to policy is an *a priori* one, in that policies are not to be based on 'tried and tested' methods. Rather policy is to be based on a logic which resembles the approach of a social planner trained in Benthamism, or even neoclassical optimization:[9]

> ... policy is the science of doing the greatest good possible at the least possible cost, according to circumstances. Therefore the problem to be resolved is one of *'maximus et minimus'*. Policy making is like drawing a curve (a parabola). The abscissa is goods, the ordinates bads. One finds the point where the least possible bad meets with the greatest possible good. This point resolves the problem, and all human problems are like this. (Galiani, 1881, volume 2, p.276)

In order to derive a solution the problem must be 'calibrated' by time and place:

> You ask if it is good to allow unrestricted exportation of wheat? This general problem is resolved only by an indeterminate equation. You then ask if

unrestricted exportation is necessary in France in the year 1773? Now the problem is defined because you have specified the country and time; and the same equation, applied to the specific case, could sometimes give you the affirmative (positive), and sometimes the negative. Policy making is thus the geometry of curves, ... as the administration of it is the simple, geometry of surfaces; the first six books of Euclid. (Galiani, 1881, volume 2, p.276)

Policy, according to Galiani, is a matter of curves and geometry: Du Pont would have quite agreed.

It is the second step of this policy-making procedure, the step of careful calibration, which David Hume would object to. Hume was doubtful that an analyst could allow for all the particulars in his reasoning: 'something is sure to happen that will disconcert his reason'. But, as a compensation, Hume was confident that these neglected particulars would not affect the results in general. Being metaphysically rationalist, Hume held that the general circumstances were enough to allow prediction of the *general* outcome of any policy.[10] Galiani, in contrast, was doubtful that particulars would not affect the result, but confident that the particular circumstances could be measured and properly accounted for. 'The means of causing this happiness, I have already said it, is always to calculate the goods and the bads, to find the best point. The uncertain is the infinitely small quantity that one mistakes in this calculation' (Galiani, 1881, volume 2, p.278). So whereas Hume was metaphysically rationalist and sceptical about the power of human reason, Galiani was metaphysically anti-rationalist and confident about the power of human reason.[11] Hume's approach is modest. Galiani's is assured.[12]

8.5 Conclusion

This chapter has argued that Quesnay's epistemology is part of the project of integration of rationalism and anti-rationalism. Quesnay was, as Weulersse wrote, as much the disciple of Locke and Condillac as Descartes and Malebranche (quoted by Lutfalla, 1981, p.43). The rest of the Physiocrats, however, ignored Quesnay's mixed epistemology of Locke and Malebranche. They instead adopted an extreme notion of justification by personal conviction, or 'evidence'. This special epistemological aspect of Physiocracy, which was briefly so powerful, left no trace on later economics. The later 19th century economists found much more to sympathize with in Turgot than, in J.B. Say's words, the 'tiresome trash' of Mercier (Say, 1865, p.xxxiv).

Quesnay was closer to his adherents in metaphysical tenets: they all shared a faith in an absolute and hierarchical natural order. It was this absolutism of Physiocracy which was challenged by Galiani, not their *a priori* method. Galiani essentially shared their method (whereas it was their method which inflamed Hume, not their presumption of a uniform general reality, which Hume shared).

The special metaphysical aspect of Physiocracy, its revival of the notion of a structure of hierarchy, may have exerted significant influence. It is plausible that it drew attention away from the alternative notion of a structure of mutual dependence, which had been so influentially advocated by Montesquieu and others, and which lent itself so well to general market equilibrium.

Notes

1　In keeping with Malebranche, Quesnay denied the Newtonian force of attraction (Quesnay, 1888, p.742).
2　One critic has suggested that Quesnay's articles in the *Encyclopédie* on 'Farmers' and 'Evidence' seem hardly to have been written by the same man (Neill, 1949, p.545). In fact, the factual aspect in 'Farmers' is consistent with the empiricist profession of 'Evidence'.
3　In this regard it is noteworthy that Condillac was a guest at Quesnay's 'entresol' at Versailles (Hecht, 1958, p.253).
4　In Quesnay's opinion, the 'divine legislation ... is manifested to men through the light of reason, cultivated through education and the study of nature, and ... admits of no other controls than the free exercise of reason itself. It is only by this free exercise of reason that men may make progress in economic science' (Quesnay, 1946, p.277). Quesnay also advises: 'Let us not seek into history of nations or into the mistakes of men, for that only presents an abyss of confusion' (Quesnay, 1946, p.273).These quotations are drawn from the last chapter of *Le Despotisme de la Chine*, the one chapter Quesnay can truly claim to be the author of. The remainder of the book, which does contain extensive historical and factual material, is almost wholly plagiarized (Quesnay, 1946, p.129).
5　Notice Quesnay is clearly inclined to a 'general theory' of illness, rather than the specific theories of illness favoured by Locke and Sydenham.
6　Quesnay's metaphysical tastes were not necessarily antipathetic to empiricism; his cherished Malebranche had said of medicine: 'Thus, our senses alone are more useful in preserving the body's health than ... theoretical medicine' (Malebranche, 1980, p.263). Leibniz, too, was doubtful of theoretical medicine (Leibniz, 1981, 426).
7　This antipathy to uniformity and stability makes a radical contrast to *Della Moneta* (see Cesarano, 1976). But even in *Della Moneta* there were some indications of Galiani's later attitude, e.g. 'one could barely hope in this world for a perpetual stability and

rigidity to be able to be established because these things are absolutely contrary to the order of things and the spirit of nature' (Galiani, 1955, p.82).

8   Diderot, Galiani's editor, missed Galiani's point entirely. His own broadside of 1770-71 (reprinted in Benot, 1954, pp.14,15) in defence of Galiani against the Physiocrats is a naive 'empiricist' one: 'in order to speak intelligently of a bakery it is necessary to have kneaded dough ... it is long experience which instructs, and all men who write on commerce without having bought or sold a needle ... expose themselves to several stupidities'. See also Strenski, 1967.

9   Galiani seems well paired with Bentham, however different their personalities. Galiani's method was one of details; this was also the method of Bentham, at least in the judgement of J.S. Mill (Mill, 1980, p.48). Galiani saw self-interest as the great directing agent of human conduct, as did Bentham. Bentham also saw himself as a relativist.

10 Galiani, in keeping with his tenet that details are everything, held that temporary shocks were more important than the general situation for the conduct of policy. It is to temporary shocks that policy should be conditioned on; policy is just 'parrying short-run movements' (Galiani, 1968, p.227).

11 An example of Galiani's confidence in his ability to prove highly specific results is his 'theorem' that money circulates only once in four years (Galiani, 1881, volume 1, p.264).

12 Hume's stance is a lesson to the defenders of general approaches to policy making: that its defence is not that particular circumstances do not matter, but that they do not matter in general.

9. Smith and the impartial synthesis

The most important economic thinkers before Smith - Mandeville, Hume, Condillac, Turgot and Quesnay - interwove in their economic analysis elements of rationalism and anti-rationalism. In Smith's work we see the most judicious synthesis of these two rival philosophies. Smith's metaphysics are distinctly rationalist, but avoid the extravagancies of Mandeville, Turgot or Quesnay. His psychology contains a strong appreciation of both human folly and human cunning. His epistemology is a compound of rationalist and anti-rationalist ideas. Smith's work can be seen as a culmination of the process this study has been concerned with.[1]

9.1 Smith on human psychology

Adam Smith (1723-1790) did not see the human mind as rational. He wrote slightingly of the 'feeble efforts of human reason' (Smith, 1937, V, i, 3, p.755).[2] He (like Hume) believed that the human mind has no relish for truth as such. Rather, the mind is in search of peace of mind. The mind finds the world is full of common order, such as bread turning into bones. 'By custom' this conception is 'smooth and easy' (Smith, 1982a, p.45). But events sometimes fall outside the common order: 'jarring, disconcordant and irregular'. It is at this point that the most advanced activity of the human mind appears: philosophy. 'Philosophy ... endeavours to introduce order into this chaos of jarring and disconcordant appearances, to allay the tumult of the imagination, and to restore it, ... to the tone of tranquillity and composure, which is both most agreeable to itself, and most suitable to is nature. Philosophy, therefore, may be regarded as one of those arts which address themselves to the imagination ...'(Smith, 1982a, p.46). Thus the philosopher is a poet, not a lover of knowledge; and philosophy is a child of the imagination, not a product of the intellect. This stress on the creative possibilities of the imagination is highly anti-rationalist.[3]

In sympathy with his deprecation of the importance of the intellect, Smith did not assume, as a matter of principle, that humankind was instrumentally rational. The greater part of men, he said, have an 'absurd presumption in their own good fortune' (Smith, 1937, I, x, 1, p.107). He used this irrationality as a source of economic explanation: why lottery tickets are purchased, why insurance is unprofitable, why soldiers are so ill paid (their 'romantic hopes' constituting a non-pecuniary wage).[4]

Nevertheless, Smith allowed that the counsel of instrumental rationality was a strong influence on most human conduct (see Hollander, 1977; Morrow, 1969 pp.72-5; Spiegel, 1979, p.45). Smith wrote that 'though the principles of common prudence do not always govern the conduct of every individual, they always influence that of the majority of every class or order' (Smith, 1937, II, ii, p.279). And Smith also used instrumental rationality as a source of explanation. Free agriculture is more efficient than slavery since the 'marginal rate of tax' on a slave's exertion is 100 per cent, while that on a free man is lower. Even the soldier is rational enough to compare his estimates of the benefits from alternative occupations.

Smith's mixed position on the role of instrumental rationality is complemented by his use of a concept of 'prudence', in place of instrumental rationality. Hutcheson had earlier defined 'prudence' (or 'wisdom') as 'the pursuing of the best ends by the best means' (Hutcheson, 1973, p.71). To Smith prudence (or 'wise and judicious conduct') consisted of the union of two qualities (Smith, 1982b, p.189). The first is the 'superior reason and understanding, by which we are capable of discerning the remote consequences of all our actions, and of foreseeing the advantage or detriment which is likely to result from them'. The second is 'self command, by which we are enabled to abstain from present pleasure or to endure present pain, in order to obtain a greater pleasure or to avoid a greater pain in some future time'.[5] In making self command a property of prudence, Smith is evidently adopting Locke's doctrine of the irrationality of positive time preference. If time preference is irrational, Smith must judge the wisdom of human conduct more harshly than would the modern neoclassical. In deriding the 'romantic hopes' of human beings Smith was throwing doubt on the wisdom of human conduct on anti-rationalistic grounds. But in supposing that time preference is irrational Smith is throwing doubt on the wisdom of human conduct on rationalistic grounds. So in Smith anti-rationalism and rationalism make a strange alliance to throw doubt on the notion that the world conducts its affairs wisely.

Smith also adopted a mixed position on several other aspects of human psychology. Is humankind active and pragmatic, or philosophic and contemplative? Humankind in Smith's view has a constant instinct to better itself (active), but the end of that betterment is 'repose' (philosophic) (Smith, 1982b, p.149). Nature has not made man fit for the Stoic vision of the contemplative life, but it has endowed him with a contemplative faculty to soften life's reversals (Smith, 1982b, p.292).

Smith's explanation of our moral judgements also supposes a mixture of rationalist and emotivist positions. The *Theory of Moral Sentiments* is built about humankind's capacity for fellow-feeling. Yet at a critical point in the *Theory* reason is brought in to buttress the impartial spectator. 'It is reason, principle, conscience, ... who calls to us ... that when we prefer ourselves so shamefully and blindly to others, we become the proper objects of resentment ...'(Smith, 1982b, p.137).

Smith's views on the origin of language again illustrate his even-handed treatment of psychological rationalism and anti-rationalism. Language, like medicine, had become in the 18th century a field of contest between rationalists and anti-rationalists (see Berry, 1974). The rationalists of the 18th century believed that speech was the product of reason. Psychological anti-rationalists found the origin of speech in natural cries (Condillac, Turgot); or in a wish for domination (Mandeville). In the *Considerations Concerning the First Formation of Languages* of 1761 Smith adopts a qualified rationalist theory of language origins.[6] To Smith the emergence of language was not a matter of natural cries, or part of a war for dominion. It was a product of the power of human reasoning *including all the limitations and imperfections of that power*. It was a product of human reason, but it was a product of the 'feeble efforts of human reason'.

Smith's method in the *Considerations* is to provide a conjectural history of language. He conjectured that the early forms of human language conformed to the low degree of reasoning of the early 'contrivers of language, whom we are not to suppose very abstract philosophers ...' (Smith, 1985, p.11). Smith painted a story of how the early languages 'evaded' sophisticated abstractions by the whole apparatus of grammar: suffixes, cases, moods. He explained many of the familiar grammatical features of language (for example, plural cases) by the lack of reasoning power in humankind. Consider qualities: in modern human languages these are commonly represented by adjectives. Adjectives may seem simple, but they are always general. 'The invention, therefore, even of the simplest nouns adjective, must have required more metaphysics than we are apt to be aware of' (Smith, 1985, p.207). He suggested that the abstract quality of gender was beyond early peoples, and so, rather than use the adjectives 'female' and 'male', female and male forms were distinguished by different nouns. Similarly, 'two' is an abstract concept, apparently too much so for the early contrivers of languages, and so the first languages had a dual case. The word 'I' is very abstract; it does not indicate a particular, neither does it indicate a class; it is a symbol whose meaning changes according to who is using it. Therefore to evade this abstraction the first languages used conjugating verbs. Prepositions such as 'of' required a 'considerable degree of abstraction' (Smith, 1985, p.210), but this abstraction was avoided by the use of genitive suffixes.[7] So Smith's picture is of language progressing with the intellectual progress of humankind; it is a picture of language waiting upon the slowly maturing intellectual faculties of humankind.

9.2 Smith on the sources of knowledge

In questions of epistemology, Adam Smith tended to a compromise position between rationalist and anti-rationalist doctrines regarding the sources of knowledge.

Anti-rationalists held that experience constituted the source of knowledge. In conformity with this claim the *Wealth of Nations* is rich in its reference to experience. This experience includes not only historical events and law, but also quantitative data. Smith may dryly confess to have 'no great faith' in political arithmetic, but this confession immediately follows his own exercise in political arithmetic (Smith, 1937, IV, v, p.501). In that exercise he sought to show that the internal corn trade was far more important to the United Kingdom than the external corn trade. He conducted a scrupulous examination of wheat prices from 1202 to 1764, including computations of running averages, in order to support his contention about the trend of wheat prices.[8]

In sympathy with his stress on experience, Smith upheld the anti-rationalist disbelief in a 'logic of discovery'. Smith, unlike Condillac, did not believe that there had been a methodological revolution in the 17th century. Smith, like Dubos, believed that, if the Moderns know more about nature than the Ancients, it is only because the Moderns have been favoured by chance discoveries. Smith in his *History of Ancient Physics* (Smith, 1982a) was a highly sympathetic critic of the ancient system of four elements: Earth, Water, Fire and Air. 'Let us not despise those ancient philosophers, for thus supposing, that these two elements [Fire and Air] had a positive levity, or a real tendency upwards ... those facts and experiments, which demonstrate the weight of the Air, and which no superior sagacity, but *chance alone*, presented to the moderns, were altogether unknown to them ...' (Smith, 1982a, p.109. Our italics).

However, Smith was not a pure anti-rationalist. Regarding the responsibility for technical knowledge, Smith shared the credit evenly between philosophers and non-philosophers. In the *Lectures on Jurisprudence* the watermill and steam engine are attributed to philosophers, while the handmill and plough are attributed to non-philosophers, as Dubos would suppose (Smith, 1978, p.492). He repeats this distribution of responsibility between practitioners and theorists in the opening pages of the *Wealth of Nations* (Smith, 1937, I, i, p.10).

On a more fundamental level, Smith could not be a pure anti-rationalist since he rejected the naive empiricist presumption that one could 'go out and see' how the world works. He rejected this presumption partly because induction, the procedure by which general truths are drawn from experience, is itself 'one of the operations of reason' (Smith, 1982b, p.319). And he rejected this presumption partly because the senses, according to Smith, were never intended by 'nature' to provide us with knowledge, but merely to assist our survival (Smith, 1982a, pp.167,168). This doctrine had been earlier advanced by Malebranche (Malebranche, 1980, p.32), an 'ingenious and sublime philosopher' according to Smith, (Smith, 1982a, p.125), who evidently shared part of Quesnay's admiration.

The senses alone cannot provide knowledge of how the world works because the chains that bind the world cannot be seen; they are *invisible*. The *invisible* is a crucial theme in Smith. On this he makes a strong contrast with Hume. Hume is a very *scenic* writer: the world is a passage of scenes. To Smith it is what is unseen which seems important. This stress on the invisible chains which bind is very rationalist, and reminiscent of the invisible and subtle fluids that performed so much work in the theories of Malebranche, Descartes and others.[9]

Smith saw at least two remedies for the problem of the invisible. The first is the least important, but the most surprising: Smith was willing to revive the doctrine of innate knowledge. Smith, like almost any Enlightenment *philosophe*, rejected the Platonic theory of innate knowledge (Smith, 1982a, pp.118-129). But, in contrast to Lockean empiricists, Smith believed nature has granted us some innate knowledge.[10] Specifically, Smith believed we have innate awareness of the connection between the visible and the tangible. Smith, following Berkeley, maintained that we do not directly perceive the distances or magnitudes of tangible objects; we only see images which by a 'language of the eyes' represent distances and magnitudes. But Smith maintained, against pure empiricists, that we have a degree of innate knowledge of the distances represented by the images our sight provides us: 'That, antecedent to all experience, the young of at least the greater part of animals possess some instinctive perception of this kind, seems abundantly evident. Almost as soon as ... chickens are hatched ... they walk about at their ease, it would seem, and appear to have the most distinct perception of all the tangible objects which surround them' (Smith, 1982a, p.161). This concession of Smith to innate knowledge has little role to play in his system, but it does indicate how far his mind was beyond the sway of Lockean precept.

The second, and much more important remedy for the problem of the invisible, is a resort to the intellect. The intellect gives us the power to hypothesize, to create in our mind connections we have not observed. Smith, with Condillac, revived hypothesis. The Mercantile System, the Physiocratic System, and his own 'liberal' system are examples of such hypothesized connections between visible objects.

But Smith, treading the prudent middle path as ever, is averse to the wrong kind of hypothesis. The wrong kind is called, as always, 'speculation'. In the manner of all empiricists, Smith indicts speculative medicine as a model of bad speculation and slights it in the *Wealth of Nations* (Smith, 1937, IV, ix, p.638).

Finally, the middle path is again trod by Smith with regard to criteria for judging hypotheses: he adopts both empirical and rationalist criteria. Gravity, the most celebrated hypothesis of his day, is a case in point. Gravity, says Smith, is a fact of daily experience: 'The gravity of matter is, of all its qualities, after its inertness, that which is most familiar to us. We never act upon it without having occasion to observe this property'. But gravity also agrees by analogy with other principles: 'The law too, by which it is supposed to diminish as it recedes from its centre, is the same which takes place in all other qualities which are propagated in rays from a centre ...'. He adds, cryptically, 'we are necessarily determined to conceive that, from the nature of the thing, it must take place' (Smith, 1982a, p.104).

To summarize, Smith valued experience, but argued that experience was not sufficient for knowledge owing to the invisibility of the chains of nature, and hypothesis must substitute.

9.3 The imaginary, the natural and the normal

Smith's esteem of hypothesis put him among rationalists, and separated him from pure empiricists. At the same time Smith accepted the empiricist warning that, since underlying causes are invisible, hypotheses about those underlying causes were prone to be false. But Smith provided this crucial addendum: hypotheses may be valuable *even if false*. So by combining the empiricist thesis of the doubtfulness of the truth of hypotheses with the rationalist thesis of the value of hypothesis, Smith arrived at a highly instrumental conception of theories. This instrumentalist conception of the role of hypothesis is advanced most distinctly in his monograph, *The Principles Which Lead and Direct Philosophical Enquiries; Illustrated by the History of Astronomy*, posthumously published in 1795.

Astronomical theories, Smith claimed, do not address 'the real chains which Nature makes use of to bind together her several operations' (Smith, 1982a, p.106), but are 'mere inventions of the imagination, to connect together the otherwise disjointed and disconcordant phaenomena of nature' (Smith, 1982a, p.106).[11] He compared them to machines, that is objects which are 'invented', rather than discovered:

> Systems in many respects resemble machines. A machine is a little system, created to perform, as well as to connect together, in reality, those different movements and effects which the artist has occasion for. A system is an imaginary machine invented to connect together in the fancy those different movements and effects which are already in reality performed. (Smith, 1982a, p.66)

The notion that astronomical theories may be useful, even if they were mere inventions of the fancy, was not a new one (e.g. King, 1970, p.155). There is a hint of astronomical instrumentalism in Condillac's *Traité des Systèmes* of 1749, of which Smith owned a copy (Condillac, 1947, volume 1, p.196).[12] Mandeville had earlier claimed that astronomical theories are just rules that make a show. In more general terms, the notion of a useful fiction was not new. Leibniz on occasion justified the 'infinitely small' of calculus as a useful fiction. Locke had suggested that medicine should treat hypotheses 'as artificial helps to a physician, and not as philosophical truths to a naturalist' (Locke, 1976, volume 4, p.630). Mini (1974) has suggested that the 'states of nature' and the 'original contracts' of 17th century political theory were not always taken literally, but were treated by some of their advocates as useful fictions.

But if Smith's advocacy of useful fictions was not a novelty, it did contrast significantly with David Hume. Hume never took much notice of the idea of useful fictions, at least in a scientific context.[13] In the Science of Man, Hume sought general truths not fictions. Smith's instrumentalism presented social science an alternative to Hume's search for general truths.

But did Smith himself extend his instrumentalism beyond natural science into his Science of Man? Could Smith have believed that his political economy was only a useful fiction? To help answer this, recall our contention that Smith's instrumentalism arose from the combination of the rationalist emphasis on the invisibility of important truth with the empiricist doubts of any knowledge of the invisible.

So, to the first question: did Smith hold important truth in the social world to be invisible? Or did Smith think that in the *social* world the real chains are *not* hidden, a view which was already latent in Locke, and became popular later in the 19th century (e.g. Cairnes, 1888)?

Certainly, Smith suggests in the *Theory of Moral Sentiments* that truth is more visible in the social world than in the physical world. He contrasts the ephemeral popularity of Mandeville's egoism with the far more enduring popularity of Cartesian astronomy: both were wrong, but the wrongness of Mandeville's system was easily seen since it concerned human reality (Smith, 1982b, p.314).[14]

However, it is indisputable that Smith did not believe, as Locke did, that 'our faculties ... plainly ... discover knowledge of ourselves'. He did not believe, as Cairnes evidently did, that a human being was readily transparent to itself. The human mind, Smith held, could not directly inspect itself. It could only inspect itself indirectly through the inspection of others.

> We can never survey our own sentiments and motives, we can never form any judgment concerning them; unless we remove ourselves, as it were, from our own natural station, and endeavour to view them as at a certain distance from us. But we can do this in no other way than by endeavouring to view them with the eyes of other people, or as other people are likely to view them. (Smith, 1982b, p.110)

So our own inner realities are not directly observable, but can only surmised about, by use of the judgements of others. Because of the inevitable faultiness of this indirect observation, Smith stresses 'the mysterious veil of self-delusion' that covers our conduct. This self-delusion, wrote Smith, is the 'fatal weakness of mankind, [which] is the source of half the disorders of human life' (Smith, 1982b, p.158). Clearly Smith did not believe that the real chains of human conduct were visible.

Still closer to the point, Smith plainly did not believe that all the forces governing market processes were visible. Actual prices (the prices of the everyday market) were moved about by invisible 'natural prices'. Natural prices were moved about by an invisible 'natural rate of profit'. This last was moved by the movement of capital, moved in turn by the 'invisible hand'. The facts 'in our way' are not enough to explain market processes; observed facts are insufficient.

But the mere invisibility of forces governing the human world does not by itself make for instrumentalism. Instrumentalism requires in addition that doctrine of useful fictions - that hypotheses about the invisible may be useful even if false. Does Smith ever employ useful fictions in his analysis of the social world (as apart from the purely and plainly literary device of the invisible hand)? Could it even be that Smith saw his views of the liberal system not as a 'discovery', but merely an invention to connect together things in the fancy? Some critics have supposed that Smith did deploy such fictions. Buckle (1904) is one. He argued that Smith used two crucial fictions: 'Selfish Man' in the *Wealth of Nations*, and 'Sympathetic Man' in the *Theory of Moral Sentiments*. This interpretation of Smith was taken up with enthusiasm by the instrumentalist advocate Vaihinger (1924, p.131) in *The Philosophy of 'As If'*. But Buckle's interpretation is debatable.[15]

There is, however, one fiction which Smith does make considerable use of in his economics: the average. The moving averages of wheat prices which he carefully computed were fictions; no one ever bought wheat at these prices.[16] But they were useful fictions in that they indicated the unobserved natural price (Smith, 1937, I, xi, 3, pp.251-5). It is true that the natural price, although unobserved, is not itself a fiction; there actually was a certain price that returned the natural rate of profit. Therefore, it may be argued, Smith's averages should be seen merely as an indicator of the perfectly real, if hidden, natural price. But this supposition is not entirely satisfactory, since Smith brings in the average to define the natural rate of profit, and therefore the natural price. Smith actually speaks of the 'natural' rate of profit and the 'average' rate of profit as synonymous: 'There is in every society or neighbourhood an ordinary or average rate both of wages and profit in every different employment of labour and stock ... These ordinary or average rates may be called the natural rates of wages, profit, and rent, at the time and place in which they commonly prevail' (Smith, 1937, I, vii, p.55).[17] The average was not merely the indicator of the natural; it was doubtful whether the natural even existed outside some fictional average. To Smith 'the normal' and 'the natural' were tied up in an impenetrable knot.[18]

We can see the significance of the normal, even if it did not concretely exist, in a theory of beauty that Smith entertains in the *Theory of Moral Sentiments*. In that theory the most beautiful is the 'middle form', regardless of whether the 'middle form' had a concrete existence:

> ... in each species of creatures, what is the most beautiful bears the strongest characters of the general fabric of the species, and has the strongest resemblance to the greater part of the individuals with which it is classed.

Monsters, on the contrary, or what is perfectly deformed, are always the most singular and odd, and have the least resemblance to the generality of that species to which they belong. And thus the beauty of each species, ...[is] in one sense the rarest of all things, because few individuals hit this middle form exactly .... (Smith, 1982b, pp.198-9)

The average is beautiful, the abnormal is monstrous. To Smith, nature was normal and the norm was natural.

The preceding paragraphs have suggested that Smith's concern with the normal, or average, was fed by the thought that the normal made contact with certain ideal (and therefore non-real) entities, such as the 'natural price'. But there was another source of his interest. Smith's preoccupation with the normal was also in part a manifestation of one of the deepest aspirations of rationalism: to explain the strange in terms of the mundane. To quote Stark, 'the typical attitude of all rationalists ... in the face of the unusual, the inexplicable, the irrational [is]: there must be a perfectly simple way for accounting for what happened or happens; behind the unusual must be found the commonplace, behind the extraordinary, the perfectly ordinary ...' (Stark, 1960, p.26). The exemplar of this rationalist model of explanation was their explanation of supposed miracles in terms of the ordinary facts of nature. Another manifestation of this rationalist model of explanation was their aspiration to explain all physical phenomena in terms of ordinary and 'intelligible' events (e.g. impact), and to avoid anything of a 'supernatural' appearance (e.g. gravitational attraction).

In the social sciences of the 18th century this rationalist urge to explain the unusual in terms of the commonplace had two significances. First, it encouraged thinkers to obtain their observational raw material from the ordinary and everyday. It encouraged in those with empiricist aspirations an attenuated empiricism, the empiricism of the commonplace. We see this in Hume and Condillac (with his own avowal of 'very common', trivial truths). And we also see it in Smith. The mundane, the everyday, the usual, what was everywhere commonly before us, was frequently cited by Smith, not the rare or unusual 'travellers' tale'. Burke observed and commended this tendency in Smith. In 1759 he wrote to congratulate Smith on his *Theory of Moral Sentiments*:

I own I am particularly pleased with those easy and happy illustrations from common Life and manners in which your work abounds more than any other that I know by far. They are indeed the fittest to explain those natural movements of the mind with which every Science relating to our Nature ought to begin. But one sees, that nothing is less used, than what lies directly our way. Philosophers therefore very frequently miss a thousand things that might be of infinite advantage, though the rude Swain treads daily on them with his clouted Shoon. (Smith, 1987, p.47)

This rationalist esteem of the commonplace as a source of explanation obviously harmonised wonderfully with the empiricist esteem of everyday experience as source of knowledge, the experience of the cook or the sailor, which Dubos, Locke and Mandeville so praised. Thus the commonplace, by serving both rationalist and anti-rationalist precepts, became one of the most popular starting points for enquiry in the 18th century.[19]

The second significance of this rationalist urge to explain the unusual in terms of the commonplace is that it encouraged prosaic explanations of social realities, and this aspect of rationalism Hume and Smith wholly shared. Thus Hume's economics was, in Veblen's characterization, the 'footsore quest for a perfectly tame explanation of things' (Veblen, 1964, p.55). More specifically, this rationalist urge encouraged a prosaic conception of human nature. A reader of the *Theory of Moral Sentiments* must be struck by the rather prosy, sedate vision the author has of the requirements of human happiness. 'What can be added to the happiness of the man who is in health, who is out of debt, and has a clear conscience?' To Smith, 'tranquillity' and 'repose' are ends of life, and 'Happiness consists in tranquillity and enjoyment' (1982b, p.149). Smith's vision of the motors of human conduct (as distinct from the requirements of human happiness) is, admittedly, rather less prosy. In its survey of human psychology the *Theory of Moral Sentiments* discovers jealousy, envy, joy and even 'mortal hatred'. But Smith saw such 'turbulence' as almost exclusively an aspect of human folly; the notion that turbulence was an excitement, and that some people sought and needed turbulence, seemed not to have impressed him.

The close connection between 'prosaic man' and economic man needs no elaboration. Marshall captured the flavour of much economics when he wrote 'Economics is the study of mankind in the ordinary business of life'. Galbraith also grasped this link of economics to the prosaic in griping, 'One reason that economics and sociology are dull is the belief that everything associated with human personality should be made as hum-drum as possible. This is science' (Galbraith, 1988, p.43).

9.4 Smith on the providential order

Smith's preoccupation with normality was also a manifestation of his adherence to a rationalist metaphysical principle: that the world is an order and not a chaos. Behind the apparent diversity there is a hidden uniformity.

Smith's belief in the existence of an underlying order is further revealed in his approach to explanation; by his preference for explanation of the world in terms of general principles rather than specific principles. He made the contrast between explanation by general principles and explanation by specifics in terms of 'Newtonian' and 'Aristotelian' methods:

> ... in Natural Philosophy or any other Science of that Sort we may either like Aristotle go over the Different branches in the order they happen to cast up to us, giving a principle commonly a new one for every phaenomenon; or in the manner of Sir Isaac Newton we may lay down certain principles known or proved in the beginning from whence we account for several Phenomena connecting all together by the same Chain. - This Latter we may call the Newtonian method is undoubtedly the most Philosophical, and in every science whether in Moralls or Natural philosophy etc., is vastly more ingenious and for that reason more engaging than the other. (Smith, 1985, p.145)

In keeping with his preference for general explanation, Smith faulted the Ancients on account of their metaphysics, not their epistemology. 'The idea of an universal mind, of a God of all, ... who governs the whole by general laws, directed to the conservation and prosperity of the whole, without regard to that of any private individual, was a notion to which they were utterly strangers' (Smith, 1982a, p.113).

But, to prudently balance his advocacy of explanation by general principles, Smith (like Hutcheson) criticized certain classical philosophers for an over-strong passion for inferring much from little.[20] Smith did not seek to derive all from one principle; but neither is he content to derive all from many. In the *Theory of Moral*

Sentiments (1982b, p.326) he described his theory of approbation as flowing from four principles: sympathy with the actor, sympathy with the acted upon, concord with general rules and the promotion of happiness.

It is doubtful if the *Wealth of Nations* can be derived from any identifiable 'four principles'. Smith obviously did not proceed by applying deduction to a small set of assumptions. This lack of deductivist method presumably prompted J.B. Say to describe it as a 'vast chaos' (quoted in Gray, 1980, p.215). But the *Wealth of Nations* actually reflects a horror of chaos, the same horror which (Smith believed) had prompted astronomical theories. But rather than remove this horror by a deductive system, the *Wealth of Nations* undertook to remove it by methodizing and ordering. And, by the standards of the time, this was no mean project: the French Enlightenment applauded methodizing and ordering (see for example, Turgot, 1973, p.51). In 1756 Smith plainly revealed his own attraction to the project of 'methodizing and ordering' by making this contrast between the capacities of the English and the French:

> It seems to be the peculiar talent of the French nation, to arrange every subject in that natural and simple order, which carries the attention, without any effort, along with it. The English seem to have employed themselves entirely in inventing, and to have disdained the more inglorious but not less useful labour of arranging and methodizing their discoveries, and of expressing them in the most simple and natural manner. (Smith, 1982a, p.245)

Smith in this paragraph might almost be describing the ambition of the book he was to commence ten years later; the *Wealth of Nations* was a 'labour of arranging and methodising' past discoveries and 'expressing them in the most simple and natural manner'. The book may have little invention in it, but it certainly 'entertains the mind with a regular succession of agreeable, interesting and connected objects' (Smith, 1982a, p.244). In Cournot's words,

> [Smith] is the first and one could say the only *classic* writer in these matters, precisely because he knew how to give several leading questions, simple in nature but long confused, a simplicity, a clarity of exposition that could barely be surpassed. (Cournot, 1872, p.96)

It is with reason that Cournot remarks that 'Smith is the least English of the economists of Great Britain, which explains his success in

France and elsewhere' (Cournot, 1872, p.96). The *Wealth of Nations* was not a 'vast chaos'. It was a testimony to the value his age placed on order, and its correlate, simplicity.

The *Wealth of Nations* was subservient to another rationalist metaphysical principle: the 'natural' order was beneficent. Whether he calls it nature, providence, the great author, the great director of universe, or God, Smith believed that the world was designed with a purpose for humankind. 'The happiness of mankind, as well of all other rational creatures, seems to have been the original purpose intended by the Author of nature when he brought them into existence' (Smith, 1982b, p.166). This providence has shown itself in the design of things: 'In every part of the universe we observe means adjusted with the nicest artifice to the ends which they are intended to produce ...' (Smith, 1982b, p.87). It even shows itself in the limited demand of the human stomach for food, which ensured that concentrated wealth does not concentrate food consumption, and produce starvation. The *Wealth of Nations* was to display this providence of the natural order in the economic sphere.

In economic terms, Smith's natural order operated through the invisible hand. The analytic core of the invisible hand was Smith's theory of markets and values. Here Smith's syncretic tendency also had material to work with, since the theory of value, too, is a topic of conflict between rationalism and anti-rationalism. Anti-rationalists, in keeping with their view that the world is a passion-infested place, see value as an expression of feeling, just as they see morals, beauty and belief as expressions of feeling. Anti-rationalists are consequently drawn to subjectivist theories of value. Rationalists decline to give significance to something so volatile and wilful as feeling.

Smith's choice of labour as a measure of value might therefore be supposed to be anti-subjectivist and rationalist. But this supposition is a misinterpretation. Smith's choice of labour as a measure of value reflects only his attempt to root value firmly in human feeling, but to avoid the heterogeneity of human feelings. How rich is a man? A man is rich, said Smith, according to the degree he can enjoy life (Smith, 1937, I, v, p.30). Consequently the value of possessing a commodity is the 'toil and trouble which it can save' its owner, a plainly subjectivist notion. Smith's concern was to find an indicator of that toil and trouble that was reliable. Smith nominated labour as such an indicator on the grounds that the toil and trouble of a unit of labour is the same 'at all times and places'. But why should the toil and trouble of a unit of labour be invariant with time and place? Smith's justification of this proposition was perhaps rooted in the Lockean notion that certain 'uneasinesses' are natural: to be hungry after being starved, to be sleepy after being awake, and to feel 'weariness, with labour' are to Locke natural uneasinesses (Locke, 1959, II, xxi, 46). These natural uneasinesses are contrasted by Locke to fantastic and irregular uneasinesses (such as the itch after riches) acquired by habit, fashion, example, education and custom. These last uneasinesses will hardly be constant over time and place. But natural uneasinesses will not vary with time and place; natural things never do! Therefore labour would be chosen by Smith as the measure of value.

This interpretation of Smith's choice of labour as a measure of value suggests that some critics (Halévy, 1928; Taylor, 1965) have overstated the difference between Smith and utility theorists (such as Hutcheson), who were quite happy to base value on 'any satisfaction, by prevailing custom or fancy'. In this interpretation, Smith's point against Hutcheson is only that value based on mere fancy will not allow meaningful comparisons of wealth across time and space, since fancy varies so much.

Nevertheless, Smith's theory of value is some distance from the utility theory of value, which was implicit in Dubos, and articulated by Galiani. Smith, in spite of what we might expect of an author who was so immersed and respectful of anti-rationalism, gives subjective factors an explicit role to play only in the matter of market values.

But Smith's treatment of market values is still an illustration of his synthesising tendency. The critical fact about market values, as far as the conflict between rationalism and anti-rationalism is concerned, is that they are highly irregular, even chaotic. An anti-rationalist would not be surprised by that phenomenon: the world is a heap, not an order; prices are relative to circumstance, and are therefore subjective, a matter of personal opinion. Rationalists, in contrast, would be disturbed; something that chaotic cannot be quite right. One rationalist response would be to conclude that since market values flicker erratically with time and place they cannot be significant. Indeed, in this rationalist response, market values are barely real: phantom-like, market values are merely the flickering shadows of something truly real. The Marxist labour theory of value is probably the best known expression of this Platonist style of value theory. In this theory of value market prices are no longer the object of explanation at all; rather they are disregarded as the frail shadows of immutable 'values', which are explained by another Platonic entity called 'labour'.

Smith's theory of value had elements of the anti-rationalist approach and the Platonist style rationalist approach. Market prices, for all their ephemeral fluctuations, were highly significant phenomena in Smith's systems; they were not phantoms. Smith's system operated through shifts in market prices inducing capital and labour to shift about the economy. At the same time, Smith held that the market price was not fundamental. Underlying the market price was a stable uniformity, the natural price, towards which the market price gravitated.

In the century following Smith, market values and natural values receded or advanced in the attention of economists according to the type of rationalist thinking that was predominate. For example, in Ricardo, an extreme rationalist, market prices are robbed of what attention Smith gave them, and natural prices dominate attention. But in neoclassical economics the natural price recedes into the background again. It has a vestigial existence in Marshallian 'long-run price', but is otherwise redundant. In neoclassical economics a given price is underlain, not by a natural price, but by the entire simultaneous interaction of preferences and transformation opportunities over millions of commodities.[21]

Thus one aspect of the transformation from classical to neoclassical value theory is a transition from a structure of hierarchy to a structure of mutual interdependence. Smith seems equivocal about the notion of a structure of mutual interdependence, equally impressed, perhaps, by the contrary positions of Montesquieu and the Physiocrats. He proposes a hierarchy of productivity of capitals (Smith, 1937, II, v), which is plainly a structure of hierarchy. He also proposes that labour is the source of all wealth, another structure of hierarchy. Yet, in what constitutes a classic expression of economic mutual interdependence, he argues that society becomes wealthy through the division of labour.

There remains one final metaphysical tenet of Smith to be dealt with: progress. In the *Wealth of Nations* Smith dwelt confidently on the ever-upward tendency of wealth in human society (1937, III, iii, p.327). Yet he also sombrely remarked that human prosperity rarely endures uninterrupted for more than 200 years (1937, III, iv, p.394). Is there another middle path here?

9.5 The Enlightenment consensus

The leading feature of Smith's methodology was its assimilation of elements from both rationalist and anti-rationalist streams of thought. This syncretic aspect of his work extended, beyond methodology, into doctrine. It is seen in his incorporation of certain elements of the Physiocratic position, without submitting to all its tenets. It is seen in his theory of value. It is also seen in the fact that some of his 'original' ideas were independently originated by other writers working on the same raw materials; for example, the 'four stages of growth' independently devised by Turgot.[22] This synthetic character is also seen in Smith's moderate position regarding the 18th century's debate over the relative importance of egotism and altruism: to Smith our benevolence is only a 'feeble spark', and yet our imagination allows us to be transported into others' situations and to restrain our egotism (Smith, 1982b, p.83).

This moderate, 'middle ground' character of Smith made him an almost stereotypical figure of his Enlightenment milieu. One proof of this is the high esteem in which he held the defining figure of the Enlightenment: Voltaire. It seems odd to bracket Smith and Voltaire; Smith seems so Augustan, so dignified, an utter contrast with the rapid, flashy and unabashable Voltaire. But in Rae's opinion 'There was no living name before which Smith bowed with profounder veneration than the name of Voltaire, and his recollections of their intercourse on these occasions [at the end of 1765] were always among those he cherished most warmly' (Rae, 1965, p.189). Smith kept a bust of Voltaire in his room. He quoted 'with apparent approval' Voltaire's remark that Hamlet was the dream of a drunken savage. (Rae, 1965, p.368). He judged Voltaire's *Mahomet* to be 'the very climax of dramatic excellence' (Smith, 1982b, p.177). He once said he could not 'pardon' Emperor Joseph II for not 'doing homage' to Voltaire. 'Reason owes him incalculable obligations', said Smith. 'The ridicule and the sarcasm which he so plentifully bestowed upon fanatics and heretics of all sects have enabled the understanding of men to bear the light of truth, and prepared them for those enquiries to which every intelligent mind ought to aspire' (Rae, 1965, p.190). Perhaps with reason Cournot describes Smith as a member of 'the school of Voltaire' (Cournot, 1872, p.96). By this membership, Smith put himself at the middle of a milieu which itself sought the calm of the midstream.

9.6 Conclusion

In methodological terms the *Wealth of Nations* amounts to a judicious compromise between rationalism and anti-rationalism. Smith's work can therefore be seen as a careful attempt to resolve the tensions between rationalism and anti-rationalism with which this study has been concerned.

But Smith's method of resolution tended to be one of roughly impartial concessions, rather than one of creative integration. This 'moderate' character of Smith's work made it popular, but imposed costs. The compromising character weakened Smith's deductivism; his assumptions were so reasonable they became diffuse, and left his 'conclusions' only weakly tied to their supposed premises.[23] Smith's 'empiricism of daily experience' is liable to Taine's criticism of the empiricism of the *philosophes*: that it mistook the commonplace for the important. Consider Smith's explanation of the huge increase in the productivity of labour over history. The greatest part of this is ascribed to the division of labour, whose benefit is in turn ascribed to the saving of time, the improvement of manual dexterity, and the 'inventions of common workmen, who, being each of them employed in some very simple operation, naturally turned their thoughts towards finding out easier and readier methods of performing it' (Smith, 1937, I, i, p.9). If there are parts of the *Wealth of Nations* that rely on the slight and insubstantial to explain great things, might this be one of them?

Finally, Smith's metaphysical tenets were fragile. His vision of a beneficent system was ultimately buttressed by the existence of a benevolent God. But God soon fell way, pushed by Robert Malthus. When God fell, how strong were the remaining arguments that the market system operated in a manner that secured the happiness of humankind?

Notes

1 This mixed aspect of Smith's methodology has encouraged some controversy over its character: it has been variously classified as 'deductivist' (Buckle, 1904, p.808), empiricist (Bitterman, 1940; Sismondi, quoted in Stark, 1944, p.72), anti-rationalist (Morrow, 1969), 'eclectic' (Pokorny, 1978) or a 'peculiar' combination of induction and *a priori* speculation (Leslie, 1870). The analysis of this chapter broadly concurs with these last two judgements.

2 We might compare this to the 'feeble spark of benevolence' that Smith allows human nature in the *Theory of Moral Sentiments*.

3 Smith's countenance of the imagination may be contrasted with Condillac's intolerance of it. Condillac ascribed all stupidity to imagination: 'The wisest man shall differ from the greatest blockhead only in this, that luckily for him the irregularities of his imagination have such things for their object as interfere but little in the ordinary course of life ...' (Condillac, 1971, p.86). This abhorrence of the imagination recalls Malebranche, and is totally contrary to Hume and Smith.

4 Viner: 'The important thing for the interpreter of Smith to note is how low down on this scale reason enters into the picture of influencing social behaviour. Under normal circumstances, the sentiments make no mistake. It is reason which is fallible' (Viner, 1972, p.78).

5 Thus prudence is a compound of 'cogitative' and 'sensitive' natures; it is the 'best head with the best heart' (Smith, 1982b, p.216). This resembles Hume's preference for an alloy of cogitative and sensitive faculties.

6 In contrast, Smith in the *Theory of Moral Sentiments* of 1759 adopted the Mandevillian view of the origins of language. 'The desire of ... directing other people ... is, perhaps, the instinct upon which is founded the faculty of speech, ... speech is the great instrument of ambition ...' (Smith, 1982b, p.336).

7 With regard to the origin of nouns, Smith appears to follow Locke and Condillac: all nouns began as proper names, which become generalized into general terms. Leibniz and Turgot claimed, in rebuttal of Locke, the opposite (Leibniz, 1981, 289): that all nouns began as general terms, some of which became particularized into proper names. This difference illustrates how rationalists and anti-rationalists differed on the question of the role of abstract terms in human thought: are they primary or secondary?

8 In a Lockean manner Smith laments that the 'proper study of experiment and observation' has been neglected by the universities in favour of a 'cobweb' of 'subtleties and sophisms' called metaphysics (Smith, 1937, V, i, 3, p.725).

9 Smith also observes that relations cannot be the object of external senses.

10 The Enlightenment empiricists comprehensively denied all inborn knowledge. Even the fear of heights in infants was ascribed by Condillac only to experience (Condillac, 1947, volume 1, p.728). Malebranche, by contrast, claims in the *Recherche* that such a fear is innate (see Condillac, 1971, p.80).

11 If the imagination is the creation by the mind of images not presented by the senses, then this stress on the role of imagination in science can be interpreted as another middle path between rationalism and anti-rationalism: a middle path between the anti-rationalists' stress on the senses and the rationalists' stress on the mind.

12 It is not implausible that Condillac's treatment of hypothesis reinforced Smith's own thoughts. To quote Meghill, 'There is also an abundance of evidence to show that Smith read the *Traité [des Systèmes]* with the deepest attention. For example, in one passage in the *Traité* Condillac discusses the history of astronomy - a history characterized, Condillac maintains, by the creation of astronomical systems that are progressively

more and more simple. The resemblance to Smith's "History of Astronomy" is so striking that one can only conclude that Smith wrote his history in an attempt to work out at greater length Condillac's insight' (Meghill, 1975, p.83). There is also the possibility of a significant influence of Turgot on Smith (see Groenewegen, 1983).

13 Hume (Hume, 1911, volume 1, p.189) did discuss how the imagination gives a 'coherence' to our perceptions of everyday life, such as the fire in a room.

14 'An author who treats of natural philosophy, and pretends to assign the great phaenomena of the universe, pretends to give us an account of the affairs of a very distant country, concerning which he may tell us what he pleases ... But when he proposes to explain the origin of our desires and affections ... he pretends to give us an account ... of our own domestic concerns ... we are incapable of passing any account which does not preserve some little regard to the truth.' (Smith, 1982b, p.314).

15 In neither the *Wealth of Nations* nor the *Theory of Moral Sentiments* is humankind benevolent. If there seems little sign of 'general fellow feeling' in the *Wealth of Nations*, there also seem to be few actions which the impartial spectator would object to.

16 Smith's use of the average is not as unremarkable as it may at first seem, since the word 'average', in the sense of arithmetical mean, is an 18th century neologism. The oldest usage of 'average' as an adjective that is recorded by the *Oxford English Dictionary* is from 1735. The oldest usage it records of 'the average' as a noun is from 1755.

17 Veblen is not impressed by this conjunction: 'the occurrence of the words "ordinary" and "average" need not be taken too seriously. The context makes it plain that the equality which commonly subsists between the ordinary and average rates, and natural rates, is a matter of coincidence not necessity' (Veblen, 1964, p.82). This remark is part of Veblen's project to paint Smith as a natural law deist, of a Physiocratic kind; surely a misrepresentation.

18 There may be a parallel between Smith's use of the average in value theory and Hume's use of 'tendency' in his theoretical history. Hume's object of inquiry in his theoretical history was the tendency of human history: he was not seeking to excavate 'deep' laws of history which supposedly had been overlaid by passing shocks. It could be argued that, in the same way, Smith's object of inquiry in value theory was the average price, not some deep underlying price which had been obscured by shocks. If this is interpretation of Smith is valid, then Smith's approach to price stands in contrast to that of Turgot, who quite clearly conceived a 'fundamental price' underlying the 'current price'.

19 In his *Reflections on Political Economy* of 1771 Pietro Verri praises those 'who by imperceptible degrees, lead our attention firmly from ordinary notions to those more remote and most important: this is the story of every science, and the genesis of every truth' (Verri, 1986, p.3). In this remark Verri summarizes the doctrine that the commonplace is the beginning of knowledge. Schumpeter commends Verri on the grounds that he 'knew how to weave fact-finding and theory into a coherent tissue: the methodological problems that agitated later generations of economists he had successfully solved for himself' (Schumpeter, 1954a, p.178). In fact, Verri's proposed solution to the fact-theory problem is wholly characteristic of his age.

20 '... Epicurus indulged a propensity, which is natural to all men, but which philosophers in particular are apt to cultivate with a peculiar fondness, as the great means of displaying their ingenuity, the propensity to account for all appearances from as few principles as possible' (Smith, 1982b, p.299).

21 There is a parallel between the disappearance of natural (or long-run) prices in modern neoclassical economics, and the disappearance of the trend (or long-run) growth rate in real business cycle macroeconomics.

22 Meek claims that Smith and Turgot devised the four stages theory (hunting, pasturage, agriculture and commerce) almost simultaneously: 'one of the most remarkable coincidences in the whole history of social and economic thought' (Meek, 1971, p.24). Turgot also shared Smith's views on the destructive influence of industrial progress on the minds of common mechanicals (Turgot, 1913, volume 1, pp.348-9).

23 Cournot's rigour is in part animated by his dissatisfaction with the low standards of proof in Smith (Cournot, 1929, p.160).

10. The synthesis dissolves

The preceding chapters have traced how economic thought in its period of origin was shaped by two alternative visions of the human world: one emphasizing order and intellect, and the other deprecating both. Early in the 18th century pure expressions of both of these approaches were attempted in economics, but they had little further issue. Instead economic thinkers, with varying degrees of success, tended to blend both visions, rather than pursue one or the other. At the close of the 18th century this syncretic tendency reached an apogee in Smith's *Wealth of Nations*, with its fusion of rationalist metaphysics and anti-rationalist psychology.

The *Wealth of Nations* was, however, an end rather than a beginning; it had many admirers, but few imitators. The *Wealth of Nations* did not provide a victory for either rationalism or anti-rationalism; and neither was it a genuine integration of the two. It was, in the main, merely a judicious compromise between these two contrary philosophies. In the following two centuries pure expressions of rationalism and anti-rationalism were reformulated and remain in contention today. This chapter draws in broad brush strokes the re-emergence of the divide between the two outlooks.

10.1 The attack of the *a priori*

Epistemologically, classical economics soon began to deviate from the middle path of Smith, and followed instead a path which emphasized intellect, introspection and deductivism. They were guided in this journey by Smith's pupil and literary executor, Dugald Stewart (1753-1828), who in turn found guidance in David Hume.

Stewart outlined his methodology in *The Elements of the Philosophy of the Human Mind*, the first volume of which was published in 1792. Stewart saw himself as a stringent empiricist; he saved his greatest praise for Bacon. But his empiricism allowed him to insist on general principles in political economy. He followed Hume in arguing that these general principles are empirical by virtue of being founded on daily experience. With specific regard to Smith's principles of political economy, Stewart repeatedly pressed that their foundation lay in daily experience:

> The premises, it is perfectly obvious, from which these [i.e. Smith's] conclusions are deduced, are neither hypothetical assumptions, nor metaphysical abstractions. They are practical maxims of good sense, approved by the experience of men in all ages of the world; and of which, if we wish for any additional confirmations, we have only to retire into our own bosoms, or to open our eyes on what is passing around us. (Stewart, 1867, p.525)

In Stewart's view anyone could, like Smith, 'open their eyes' and see that it is folly for a shoemaker to make his own clothes. So anyone may justly conclude with Smith that 'what is prudence in the conduct of every private family, can scarcely be folly in that of a great kingdom'. So although Smith may be said 'in one sense, to indulge in theory' when he argues for free-trade, in a more 'philosophical sense' he is relying on 'those maxims of expediency, of which every man may verify the truth by his own daily observation' (Stewart, 1867, p.135). Theory to Stewart is really just the facts of everyday life.

Because the foundation of economic principles is direct and everyday experience, Stewart firmly repudiated the notion that theories are essentially hypothetical. Stewart pushed Hume's ideas about the factual roots of general principles to justify an iron-clad confidence in political economy. In an irony which would cause the paradoxical philosopher no surprise Stewart pressed these ideas to vindicate that special object of Hume's rage: Physiocracy. The Physiocrats in Stewart's opinion 'established with demonstrative evidence' some of 'the most important principles of political economy...' (Stewart, 1867, p.132).

So confident was Stewart in the factuality of theory that he issued a scandalized reprimand of Smith over his stress in the *History of Astronomy* on the hypotheticality of theories:

> Mr Smith himself has been led ..., into expressions concerning the Newtonian discoveries, which seem to intimate, that, although he thought them far superior, in point of ingenuity, to anything the world had seen before, yet, that he did not consider them as so completely exclusive of a happier system in times to come, ...

If the view which I have given of Lord Bacon's plan of investigation be just, it will follow, that the Newtonian theory of gravitation, ... is as little liable to be supplanted by the labours of future ages, as the mathematical conclusions of Euclid and Archimedes. (Stewart, 1867, pp.462-4)

By rejecting the need for hypotheticality in the Science of Man, Stewart was developing Hume, rather than Smith. To be sure, the sceptical Hume may have baulked at Stewart's claims to certainty regarding the conclusions of political economy. But in his assumption of a plain observational foundation of the general claims (or 'theory') of political economy Stewart is in a line of descent from Hume, rather than Smith.[1]

Because Stewart believed his 'political economy of everyday experience' was not hypothetical he denied the pretensions of the political arithmeticians ever to stand in judgement of the doctrines of political economists. In support of this stand Stewart instanced the debate over the economic efficiency of slavery. From the everyday fact that labour acts in its own interest, Smith had argued that slave labour is more costly than free labour. Certain political arithmeticians had disputed this with facts of American slavery. But a better appreciation of these far-away facts, said Stewart, had vindicated Smith and political economy. The lesson is that the facts of everyday life, those which we understand and are so sure of, are a much better basis of principles than 'facts' about things which are not part of our everyday life. Stewart pressed the attack on political arithmeticians a stage further:

The facts which the political philosopher professes to investigate are exposed to the examination of all mankind; and while they enable him, like the general laws of physics, to ascertain numberless particulars by synthetic [i.e. deductive] reasoning, they furnish the means of estimating the credibility of evidence resting on the testimony of individual observers. (Stewart, 1867, p.523)

Therefore, concluded Stewart, '... instead of appealing to political arithmetic as a check on the conclusions of political economy, it would often be more reasonable to have a recourse to political economy as a check on the extravagancies of political arithmetic' (Stewart, 1867, p.523). Here one sees the critical *a priori* turn of Stewart. One sees how an ostensibly empiricist thinker actually insulates theory from empirical check. Instead of the 'data rejecting the model', it is now a case of 'the model rejecting the data'.

The justification of Stewart's scepticism of political arithmeticians also had its roots in Hume. It was Hume, recall, who had scoffed at the 'chimerical calculations' of political arithmeticians concerning the balance of trade. And Stewart's use of principles to do a 'quality check' on the facts of political arithmeticians formed an exact parallel to Hume's recommended method of detecting forgery in historical documents; to judge, given our knowledge of the *general character* of human motivations, whether the reported circumstances 'could ever induce' the reported actions (Hume, 1975, p.84).

There is one other argument in favour of 'theory' which Stewart borrows from Hume: the notion that conclusions based on general principles are true in general, if not true universally. Stewart buttresses his use of general principles by extensive quotation from Hume's 'profound reflections' on this argument in favour of general principles (Stewart, 1867, pp.357,399).

But Stewart's advocacy of theory in the guise of empiricism is not merely the result of an exaggeration of some of David Hume's doctrines. Stewart's false empiricism is just one example of a general tendency of Enlightenment thought. The Enlightenment, standing in the shadow of the victory of the 'empirical' Newtown over a 'theoretical' Descartes, professed and aspired to an empirical method. But that aspiration was not fulfilled. Their stress on the commonplace as the proper source of observation, along with their rejection of the exotic 'travellers' tale', shrivelled their empiricism.[2] The weakness of their inductive methods encouraged them to resort to theory. Their denial that there was something called 'theory' that was legitimately distinct from empirics, actually facilitated that shift to theory, since that denial left them less able to distinguish theory and fact. For these reasons there is a strong tendency in the 18th century for supposed empiricists to adopt theoretical methods. We have seen this in Condillac, Turgot and Quesnay, as well as Hume.

What really distinguished Stewart's approach from that of Condillac, Turgot, and Quesnay was that his was taught to the English political economists of the early 19th century. Stewart was the pre-eminent British philosopher at the beginning of that century. He held the Chair of Moral and Political Philosophy at Edinburgh University. In 1793 and 1798 he gave the only lectures in political economy in any university in Britain in that decade (Rashid, 1985, p.251). His student audience included J.R. McCulloch and James Mill. Mill remained what Halévy describes as a 'disciple' of Stewart in psychology until 1808 (Halévy, 1928, p.447). Mill shared Stewart's superconfidence in theory, and his distress at its misidentification with mere hypothesis.[3] (See also De Marchi, 1983, on Stewart's influence on James Mill.) Stewart was also carefully read by Richard Whateley, who in turn was one of the greatest influences on Nassau Senior (Rashid, 1985, p.237). Stewart drew distinguished foreign visitors, including J.B. Say in December 1814, whose methodological views seem quite in harmony with Stewart's (Halévy, 1928, p.272).[4]

Overall, one may say that Stewart's 'function' was to supply to economists of the early 19th century an empiricist adaptation of the rationalist requirement that knowledge derives from truths 'so evident they need only to be understood to be believed'. Knowledge now derived from truths 'so evident that they only have to be noticed to be believed'. By supplying this adaptation Stewart cleared a path for the *a priori* phase in English political economy of the first half of the 19th century. This was the period in which economics managed to combine the empiricist disdain for mere hypothesis, with the rationalist disdain for mere facts. This was the period in which Ricardo, echoing Stewart, repudiated 'practical' thinkers without theory, since they were unable to 'sift' their facts: 'They are credulous and necessarily so, because they have no standard of reference' (Ricardo, 1952, volume 3, p.181). This was the period in which Ricardo claimed his theoretical conclusions were as 'demonstrable as any of the truths of geometry' (Ricardo, 1952, volume 8, p.390), and J.S. Mill pronounced that the method of political economy must be *a priori* (Mill, 1844, p.143). Never before, or since, had English political economy been so confidently theoretical, but *never had it been so certain it was factual*. But this irony is quite explicable: the supposed factuality of their theories, as taught by Stewart, removed any caution in the deployment of theory.

The Hume-Stewart method of deductive systemizing based on 'robust common sense' did not disappear with classical economics. It was retained by some later neoclassicals. It was given a vigorous defence in Robbins's *Essay on the Nature and Significance in Economic Science*, first published in 1932. Without ever referring to Stewart, Robbins repeats Stewart's thesis that the foundation of economic theory lies in everyday experience. The foundation of value theory, for example, is in common experience. Its basis is the 'elementary fact of experience' that we have preference orderings (Robbins, 1935, p.75). The foundation of the law of diminishing returns is the 'obvious fact' that different factors of production are imperfect substitutes for one another (Robbins, 1935, p.76). These propositions are 'simple and indisputable facts of experience' (Robbins, 1935, p.78). In Robbins's judgement these postulates are 'so much the stuff of our everyday experience that they have only to be stated to be recognised as obvious' (Robbins, 1935, p.79). How very like Descartes's claim that the principles of his physics are 'so evident they need only to be understood to be believed' (Descartes, 1985, volume 1, p.145).

This method of deduction from 'robust common sense' was also employed by the principal critics of neoclassical economics. Keynes's *General Theory* is reminiscent of Ricardo in method (see Schumpeter, 1954a, pp.473,1171). It was quite in keeping with this deductivist method for Keynes, shortly after the *General Theory,* to dismiss the fledgling practice of econometrics as a method 'neither of discovery nor criticism' (Keynes, 1939, p.560).

But it was at about the time of the *General Theory* that theoretical economics came under pressure from *a posteriori* critiques. In the 1930s there was something of an empiricist revival in Anglo-American economics (e.g. Hutchison, 1938; Beveridge, 1937). Among these empiricist critics were some (for example, Hall and Hitch, 1939) who, as if they were taking Stewart's programme literally, collected and attended to the common maxims of business life. Another pressure on the *a priori* method was applied by the Keynesian revolution. Although Keynes's method was perfectly *a priori,* the new theory was ostensibly based on the inability of neoclassical theory to meet the facts.[5]

Two methodological developments of the mid-20th century may be seen as responses to this mid-century tension between the *a priori* and the *a posteriori*. Milton Friedman's 'Methodology of Positive Economics' is one such development: its simultaneous disregard for the realism of assumptions and stress on the accuracy of prediction combines to some degree the *a priori* and the *a posteriori*. (Notice that the pressure of the same tension resulted in instrumentalism in both

Smith and Friedman.) Another such development was the spread of falsificationism in economics which, by stressing the necessity for both theory and empirics, provided a coalition of the two.

Both the Friedmanite and falsificationist defences of theory repudiated the notion that theory had a foundation in 'daily experience'. To Popperians the idea that premises were established by daily experience would have offended the essential hypotheticality of theory. Friedman threw ridicule on surveys of the daily conduct of business men, and disdained attempts at realistic assumptions. It was in the post-war period of 'positive economics' that empiricism of everyday life was displaced by the formal inferential apparatus of modern econometrics. It was in this period that 'everyday experience' became merely 'anecdotal evidence', or even worse, 'casual empiricism'.

However, these instrumentalist and falsificationist defences of theorizing were not especially successful: the 'fictions' that economists had slowly developed over the preceding 200 years turned out either to have no predictions (and therefore be not useful) or to have wrong predictions (also not useful).

One response to the apparent predictive failure of theories was to withdraw into a highly rationalist method. This method emphasized explanation, rather than prediction, claimed that prediction without explanation is impossible in any case (the Lucas Critique), and sought explanation from a small set of principles. This tendency was manifested in the increasingly 'puristic' applications of neoclassical theory, such as 'new classical' economics.

Karl Brunner (in Klamer, 1984, p.195) with reason detected a 'Cartesian tradition' at the base of new classical economics: 'The Cartesian tradition insisted that all statements be derived from a small set of "first principles". "Cogito ergo sum" and everything else follows. This idea has had a strong influence on philosophy but also on the program of new classical economics best represented by Neil Wallace. Anything not derived from "first principles" does not count as knowledge.' The horror expressed by new classicals of the 'brute fact' or the 'ad hoc' is reminiscent of 17th century rationalism. The new classical requirement that any medium of exchange be endogenously derived from the 'primitives' of preferences and technologies is one example of their rationalist urge to derive everything from a narrow but general foundation of first principles.

But what would qualify as a first principle for these new rationalists? To answer this problem, new classical economics gave new life to the old, rationalist requirement that ideas be 'clear and distinct'. Lucas has identified as the essential feature of his models that the decision problems which the decision maker faces are 'clear' (quoted in Howitt, 1986, p.106). Howitt (1986) characterizes the new classical methodology as requiring the 'clear and precise' articulation of optimization and equilibrium. Brunner also draws attention to this emphasis on precise concepts in the new classical precepts concerning monetary theory: 'You are not allowed to talk about money if you have not derived from "first principles" a specification of all the items that are money' (in Klamer, 1984, p.195).

The new classical insistence on the 'clear and precise' contrasts with the importance Keynes gave to what he called 'fluffy thoughts'. Skidelsky notes that 'Keynes always pleaded for "charity" towards factual or logical mistakes or obscurities, since much the most important thing was to get the drift of the argument, to consider whether it had value' (Skidelsky, 1992, p.424).[6] The division between Keynes and the new classicals over 'clear and distinct' ideas is not merely incidental to their doctrinal disagreements. Howitt (1986) contends that the new classical requirement of clarity and precision gave an advantage to new classicals over Keynesians since the conception of equilibrium is clearer than the conception of disequilibrium.[7]

In the light of the frustration with 'positive economics' and puristic neoclassical economics of clear and precise ideas, the return to 'daily experience' has also been mooted (see McCloskey, 1983, pp.514-5). Such a revival would have merits. One of the virtues of the empiricism of daily life is that it is respectful of the wealth of our experience. The so-called 'empiricist' who demands econometric evidence before he will credit a downward sloping demand curve for cannabis is not respectful of experience; he is ignoring our general experience that we are disposed to buy less of any commodity the more expensive it becomes.

However, a sceptic is entitled to doubt that everyday experience will provide a solid empirical foundation of the general principles of any deductive system. This is because everyday experience reduces to the 'personal experience' of the individual economic analyst. By two paths this personal experience is prone to undermine the empirical foundation of general principles. First, personal experience can become introspection, the 'looking into the bosom' which Stewart mentions. Such an introspective method clearly spells the end of the empirical foundation of general principles.[8] Second, personal experience can become the externally observable but specific experience of the economic analyst. This is a problematic foundation for general principles since some part of the truths that the economic analyst has learnt by personal experience will be true only in the particular situations that the economic analyst has experienced. The theorist presumably wishes to work with those truths which are true in wide variety of situations, spanning cultures, continents and centuries. But how can one know, from one's own personal experience, those truths that are true in such a wide variety of situations? The scientific identification of general truths seems to lead to formal statistical methods, and away again from personal aspects of experience.

The danger in the method of everyday experience is that, instead of a scientific attempt to cull general truth from varied experience, it will lead every person to erect his own 'theory' on his own particular experience. Malthus saw this danger clearly, in complaining of the practical man who '... when from ... the management of his own little farm, ... draws a general inference, ... then at once erects himself into a theorist; and is the more dangerous, because ... that partial experience ... is no foundation whatever for a just theory ...' (quoted in Harvey-Phillips, 1983, p.205). Malthus would be little surprised that the appeal to everyday experience is today commonly used by various 'neo-mercantilists' to justify their contentions hostile to general principles.

However the error with which Malthus faults the practical man could be rebutted against the economic theorist, who believes himself to be using principles based on the general element of everyday experience. To what extent is this theorist genuinely drawing on the general element of everyday experience, and to what extent is he overgeneralizing, by falsely assuming that his experience applies to societies of which they have no knowledge?

In summary, Stewart's attempt to wed fact to theory, by reasoning on the basis of everyday 'truths', seems to spell either the end of fact or the end of theory.

10.2 The advance of rational economic man

Of all the thinkers examined in this book, none supposed that humankind was rational in the instrumental sense. Smith was no exception to this. Two hundred years later the situation is quite the reverse: rational economic man is the fundamental principle of economic theory. How has this happened?

This huge shift could be seen as a response to a vulnerability of Smith's invisible hand. Smith, and probably other theists like Condillac and Turgot, ultimately sustained their belief in the ideal workings of the system on the supposition that the world had been designed by 'the designer' in a beneficent fashion. Following Hutcheson and Mandeville, they believed that the human order ultimately rested on certain passions which had been contrived by God, and planted in human nature, to support that order. But the Enlightenment had effected the rapid decay of the prestige of religious justifications, however remote, of human affairs. When providence could not even distantly be used to analyse economic affairs, what alternative arguments might establish the beneficence of the free market system?

One solution would be to abandon their assumption of a passionate human nature and base the beneficent operation of the system on the prudence and foresight in human behaviour. That is, one could revive the still-born project of Leibniz's 'science of happiness', and suppose human beings knew this science. To put it another way, one could put one's faith in the wisdom of man quietly tending his garden, rather than the wisdom of the Maker designing his universe (or the Legislator designing his utopia). In the 19th century economics drifted into this 'strategy', and adopted rationality in the instrumental sense. This radical shift was not made consciously, but it was slowly felt towards. And the change was very slow: in the 1930s Robbins was still resisting (against Joan Robinson) the suggestion that economics is the study of the *rational* allocation of scarce means between multiple ends: the adjective, he held, was too restrictive (Robbins, 1935, p.91).

This drift towards instrumental rationality reached a climax with the new classicals of the 1980s. In two of their premises, in particular, their unconscious revival of the rationalism of Descartes and Leibniz is evident. First, their assumption of a 'democracy of intellect'. Rational expectations implies that everyone is equal in reasoning powers. Everyone is rational, and it is impossible for someone to be 'more' rational than others. So everyone solves problems equally well. No one is intelligent, no one is stupid, no one is insane. However unsatisfactory this assumption of the 'democracy of intellect' may be, it finds close parallels in the assumptions of Descartes and Leibniz on the uniformity of human intellect.[9] Second, the new classical assumption of the '*a priori* nature of rationality' is also an unwitting revival of 17th century rationalist doctrine. In new classical economics, no one learns reasoning behaviour, consciously or unconsciously. No one has a fallacy pointed out to them. No one ever has their own powers of inference improved by exposure to others. One just arrives in the world rational and stays that way.[10] This assumption is plainly antagonistic to Locke's and Mandeville's stress on reason as something acquired.

The psychological rationalism of neoclassical economics has not been free of criticism. One strand of this criticism consists of formal tests of this assumption (see Thaler, 1992). Another weakness of psychological rationality is that it assumes that conditional probabilities of events are known. How this knowledge is arrived at is mysterious. Nobody has developed a really successful inductive logic that is free of arbitrary 'priors'. Whether events can even be rationally attributed probabilities, but must exist in a realm of 'uncertainty' (in the sense of Knight), is also unclear. These difficulties with *logical* rationality have been entirely ignored by economists. At the very beginnings of classical economics, Hume placed the problem of knowledge at the centre of the Science of Man, but Hume's lead has been ignored. The one exception, perhaps, is Keynes, who paid attention to the economic consequences of the lack of any theory of rational belief, and used this lack to argue against the existence of a well-contrived order.[11]

But the 18th century also contained the seed of another foundation of a well-contrived order in the world: cultural evolution. The theory of adaptation to circumstance by competition and selection might evade the challenges to rationalist psychology and epistemology. But the exploitation of this idea has only recently begun.

There is also another solution to the 'problem' of finding a foundation for the beneficent order: simply abandon the idea of a beneficent order. Keynes argued for this. But his large success was only temporary. Across the range of economists the rationalistic mind-set retains strength: the very language of economic 'systems' and economic 'functions' speaks of a presumption of order. And, in any case, even Keynes never denied the possibility of a beneficent order: he claimed only that it would have to be consciously created by a wise elite. Keynes's outlook is a re-expression of the yearning for Montesquieu's wise Legislator.

10.3 The ascendancy of general principles

The other metaphysical tendency of the Smithian synthesis was a belief that the greatest part of reality could be expressed by a small number of general truths. This sense of uniformity of the world was entirely accepted by most political economists. The relativism that had found nourishment in Locke, and expression in Montesquieu, was wholly discarded.[12]

This 'uniformitarian' aspect of classical economics is one aspect of its methodology that has endured into the late 20th century. It survives in almost all economic doctrines (neoclassical, Keynesian, Post-Keynesian, Austrian). They are all rationalist in their vision of a uniform nature of reality: they all subscribe to 'general theories', and propose to explain multiplicity by a few principles, which apply very broadly.

But, after three centuries of search, how much knowledge of general truths do economists have? Opinions on this will differ. An advocate of general theories would maintain that, even if satisfactory general theories have not yet been found, they will be found. But why should one assume they even exist? Scientific progress has not always consisted of moving to more general propositions: medicine in its maturity abandoned general theories of illness in favour of specific theories. Further, even if general truths do exist, why should they ever be found merely because they are being sought? A confidence in research is a rationalist notion, premised on the existence of a logic of discovery, and on a relish for truth in human beings. A doubter would claim that a logic of discovery is unknown in economics. We must await knowledge to arrive by chance. And even if it did arrive, would we accept it? Does economic inquiry have a relish for truth? Is economic research a search for truth, or a way of hiding from it? Are there good grounds for a belief in progress in economic knowledge?

In 1793, at the close of the period with which this study has been concerned, Condorcet, in his *Progress of the Human Mind*, praised the rapid advance of economic knowledge over the previous century, and exalted in the unlimited possibilities of improvement in human welfare. A few years later Malthus shattered the dogma of unlimited progress in living standards. This dogma is one doctrine of the Enlightenment which has not been retained; on the contrary, economists in the 20th century have periodically been gripped by anxiety about economic progress. Yet the assumption of progress in economic knowledge appears as largely unquestioned today as it was in the mind of Condorcet.

Notes

1 Some of Stewart's confidence in the factuality of principles presumably derives from the doctrines he absorbed from his philosophic mentor, Thomas Reid (1710-1796), the originator of the Scottish school of 'philosophy of common sense'. In his *Essays on the Intellectual Powers of Man* Reid displays a scorn for hypothesis even stronger than Stewart's. In Reid's judgement 'discoveries have always been made by patient observation, by accurate experiments, or by conclusions drawn by strict reasoning from observations and experiments. ... As this is a fact confirmed by the history of philosophy in all past ages, it ought to have taught men, long ago, to treat with just contempt hypotheses in every branch of knowledge, and to despair of ever advancing real knowledge in that way' (Reid, 1785, p.49). Reid dedicated the *Essays* to Stewart 'not only on account of a friendship begun in early life on your part ... but because if these Essays have any merit you, have a considerable share in it, having ... favoured me with your observations on every part of them' (Reid, 1785, p.iii).

2 Stewart's scepticism of the political arithmeticians echoed the Enlightenment's distrust of 'travellers' tales', something which Stewart shared. Stewart reproved Locke for his 'credulity in the admission of extraordinary facts, of which he has given so many proofs in the first book of his *Essay*, and which seems to have been the chief defect in his intellectual character' (quoted in Locke, 1959, volume 1, p.448).

3 James Mill: 'But, unhappily, the word Theory has been perverted to denote an operation very different from ... VIEWING-OBSERVING ... ; an operation which essentially consists in SUPPOSING, AND SETTING DOWN MATTERS SUPPOSED AS MATTERS OBSERVED. Theory, in fact, has been confounded with hypothesis ...' (Mill, 1869, volume 2, p.403).

4   J.B. Say: 'Nothing can be more idle than the opposition of *theory* to *practice*! What is theory, if it be not a knowledge of the laws which connect effects with their causes, or fact with facts?' (Say, 1865, p.xxi).

5   Keynes's work also reflected his feeling that the point of economics is to provide cures for problems. The pragmatic Locke would have wholeheartedly agreed. Samuelson's pleased assertion that economics had finally become useful is another expression of Keynes's feeling (Samuelson 1959).

6   'Keynes's most acid controversies after the publication of his *Treatise on Money* were with critics like Hayek who, he felt, missed what he was driving at in order to trip him up on logical points' (Skidelsky, 1992, p.424).

7   Howitt claims the new classical methodology 'forces the proponent of active stabilisation policy to explain the precise nature of the impediments to transacting and communication that prevent private arrangements from exhausting all gains from trade, without forcing the defender of laissez-faire to address with any rigour the reciprocal Keynesian question of how exactly the economic system manages to overcome all the obvious coordination problems that stand in the way of attaining the state of equilibrium that he is postulating' (Howitt, 1986, p.108).

8   McCloskey, an advocate of daily experience, displays this tendency to introspection: 'Take for instance the law of demand. He [an economist] may reasonably be persuaded of it better than he is that the earth goes round the sun, because ... he has the astronomical facts only from the testimony of people he trusts ... The economic fact he has mostly from looking into himself and seeing it sitting there'(McCloskey, 1982, p.512).

9   See for example the opening sentence of Descartes's *Discours de la Méthode*; 'Good sense is the best distributed thing in the world ...' (Descartes, 1985, volume 1, p.111). See also Hobbes, 1962, p.141.

10   These propositions are probably connected. The *a priori* nature of rationality is necessary for universal rationality, since universal rationality is unlikely to occur if rationality has to be acquired *a posteriori*.

11   Keynes had a considerable interest in Hume. See Chanier (1992) for scrutiny of the Hume-Keynes connection.

12   We see this passion for uniformity in Condorcet's raging against Montesquieu's chapter on 'Ideas of Uniformity' in the 29th book of the *Esprit des Lois*. In a telling passage Condorcet vents his vexation at Montesquieu's indifference to proposals to make uniform the system of weights and measures: 'What has been proposed in this regard, with the universal approval of all enlightened men, is to decide on a measure, fixed and invariable, that can always be retrieved; to employ it to obtain measures of weight, area capacity and weight ... ' (Condorcet, 1968, volume 1, p.377). A 'fixed and invariable' measure; how reminiscent this is of Ricardo's strange quest for a fixed and invariable measure of value. Ricardo's fascination for the uniform and absolute, as opposed to the variable and relative, is one mark of the silent spell which 18th century rationalism held over him. (See Crosland, 1972, for an account of the 18th century's search for 'fixed and invariable' units of physical measurement.)

Bibliography

Aspromourgos, Tony (1986), 'Political Economy and the Social Division of Labour: the Economics of Sir William Petty', *Scottish Journal of Political Economy*, vol. 33.

Aspromourgos, Tony (1988), 'The Life of William Petty in Relation to his Economics: A Tercentenary Interpretation', *History of Political Economy*, vol. 20.

Barratt, Glynn R. (1973), 'The Melancholy and the Wild: A Note on MacPherson's Russian Success', in H.E. Pagliaro (ed.), *Racism in the Eighteenth Century*, Case Western Reserve University Press, Cleveland.

Bassett, Gilbert W. (1987), 'The St. Petersburg Paradox and Bounded Utility', *History of Political Economy*, vol. 19.

Bayle, Pierre (1734), *The Dictionary Historical and Critical of Mr Peter Bayle*, J.J. Knapton, London.

Becker, Carl Lotus (1932), *The Heavenly City of the Eighteenth-Century Philosophers*, Yale University Press, New Haven.

Beeson, David (1992), 'Maupertuis: An Intellectual Biography', *Studies on Voltaire and the Eighteenth Century*, vol. 299.

Benot, Y. (1954), 'Un Inédit de Diderot', *La Pensée*, May/June 1954.

Bentham, Jeremy (1843), *The Works*, William Tait, Edinburgh.

Bernoulli, Daniel (1954), 'Exposition of a New Theory on the Measurement of Risk', *Econometrica*, vol. 22.

Berry, Christopher J. (1974), 'Adam Smith's Considerations on Language', *Journal of the History of Ideas*, vol. 35.

Beveridge, W. (1937), 'The Place of the Social Sciences in Human Knowledge', *Politica*, vol. 2.

Bitterman, H.J. (1940), 'Adam Smith's Empiricism and the Law of Nature', *Journal of Political Economy*, vol. 48.

Bonno, Gabriel (1950), 'Une Amitié Franco-Anglaise du XVIIe Siècle: John Locke et L'abbé du Bos', *Revue de Littérature de Comparée*, vol. 24.

Bremner, Geoffrey (1983), 'The Impossibility of a Theory of Evolution in Eighteenth Century Thought', *Studies on Voltaire and the Eighteenth Century*, vol. 216.

Brunet, Pierre (1929), *Maupertuis. Étude Biographique*, Librairie
Scientifique Albert Blanchard, Paris.

Buckle, Henry Thomas (1904), *Introduction to the History of
Civilisation in England*, George Routledge and Sons, London.

Cairnes, J.E. (1888), *The Character and Logical Method of Political
Economy*, Macmillan, London.

Caramaschi, Enzo (1959), 'Du Bos et Voltaire', *Studies on Voltaire
and the Eighteenth Century*, vol. 10.

Cassirer, Ernst (1951), *The Philosophy of the Enlightenment*, trans. by
Fritz C.A. Koelin and James P. Pettegrove, Princeton University
Press, Princeton.

Cesarano, Fillipo (1976), 'Monetary Theory in Ferdinando Galiani's
Della Moneta', *History of Political Economy*, vol. 8.

Chanier, Paul, (1992), 'Un Exemple de Critique Philosophique
Appliquée à la Théorie Économique: Hume, Keynes et les
Classiques', *Économie Appliquée*, vol. 45.

Condillac, E.B de (1947), *Oeuvres Philosophiques de Condillac*, ed.
by Georges Le Roy, Presses Universitaires de France, Paris.

Condillac, E.B. de (1953), *Lettres Inédits à Gabriel Cramer*, ed. by G.
Le Roy, Presses Universitaires de France, Paris.

Condillac, E.B. de (1971), *An Essay on the Origin of Human
Knowledge*, Scholar Facsimiles and Reprints, trans. by Thomas
Nugent, Gainesville, Florida.

Condillac, E.B. de (1979), *Logic*, trans. by W.R. Albury, Paris Books,
New York.

Condillac, E.B. de (1980), 'Les Monades', *Studies on Voltaire and the
Eighteenth Century*, vol. 187, ed. by Laurence L. Bongie.

Condorcet, Antoine Nicolas de (1968), *Oeuvres*, Friedrick Frommann
Verlag, Stuttgart-Bad Cannstatt.

Cournot, A. (1872), *Considerations Sur La Marche Des Idées et Des
Événements Dans les Temps Modernes*, Hachette, Paris.

Cournot, A. (1929), *Researches into the Mathematical Principles of
the Theory of Wealth*, trans. by Nathanial T. Bacon, New York,
Macmillan.

Cranston, Maurice (1957), *John Locke - A Biography*, Longmans
Green and Co., London.

Crosland, M. (1972), '"Nature" and Measurement in Eighteenth-Century France', *Studies on Voltaire and the Eighteenth Century*, vol. 87.

Davison, Rosen (1985), 'Diderot et Galiani: Étude d'une Amitié Philosophique', *Studies on Voltaire and the Eighteenth Century*, vol. 237.

Descartes, René (1985), *The Philosophical Writings of Descartes*, trans. by John Cottingham, Robert Stoothoff and Dugald Murdoch, Cambridge University Press, Cambridge.

Dewhurst, Kenneth (1963), *John Locke (1632-1704) Physician and Philosopher: A Medical Biography*, Wellcome Historical Medical Library, London.

Dewhurst, Kenneth (1966), *Dr Thomas Sydenham (1624-1689). His Life and Original Writings*, University of California Press, Berkeley.

Dubos, Jean-Baptiste (1704), *Les Intérêts de l'Angleterre Malentendus Dans la Guerre Présente*.

Dubos, Jean-Baptiste (1967), *Réflexions Critiques sur la Poésie et sur la Peinture*, Slatkine Reprints, Geneva.

Dugas, René (1955), *A History of Mechanics*, trans. by J.R. Maddox, Routledge and Kegan Paul, London.

Du Pont de Nemours, Pierre Samuel (1955), *On Economic Curves*, ed. by Henry W. Spiegel, Johns Hopkins University Press, Baltimore.

Du Pont de Nemours, Pierre Samuel (1984), *The Autobiography of Du Pont de Nemours*, trans. by Elizabeth Fox-Genovese, Scholarly Resources, Wilmington.

Edwards, C.H. (1979), *The Historical Development of Calculus*, Springer-Verlag, New York.

Eloy, N.F.S. (1973), *Dictionnaire Historique de la Médecine*, Culture and Civilisation, Brussels.

Endres, T. (1985), 'The Function of Numerical Data in the Writing of Graunt, Petty and Davenant', *History of Political Economy*, vol. 17.

Fellman, E.A. and J.O. Fleckstein, (1970), 'Daniel Bernoulli', *Dictionary of Scientific Biography*, Scribner, New York.

Fletcher, F.T.H. (1937), 'The Influence of Montesquieu on English Political Economists', *Economic History*, vol. 3.

Fletcher, F.T.H. (1939), *Montesquieu and English Politics (1750-1800)*, Edward Arnold, London.

Foley, V. (1973), 'An Origin of the Tableau Economique', *History of Political Economy*, vol. 5.

Formigari, Lia (1974), 'Language and Society in the Late 18th Century', *Journal of the History of Ideas*, vol. 35.

Fox-Genovese, Elizabeth (1976), *The Origins of Physiocracy: Economic Revolution and Social Order in Eighteenth Century France*, Cornell University Press, Ithaca.

Galbraith J.K., (1988), 'A New Theory of Thorstein Veblen', in B.S. Katz and R.E. Robbins (eds) *Modern Economic Classics-Evaluation in Time*, Garland, New York.

Galiani, Ferdinando (1881), *L'Abbé F. Galiani Correspondance*, ed. by Luciu Perey and Gaston Maugras, Calmann-Lévy, Paris.

Galiani, Ferdinando (1955), *De la Monnaie*, trans. by G.H. Bousquet and J. Crisafulli, Marcel Rivère, Paris.

Galiani, Ferdinando (1968), *Dialogues Entre M. Maquis De Roquemaure, et Ms. Le Chevalier Zanobi*, ed. by Philip Koch, Vittorio Klostermann, Frankfurt.

Gellner, Ernest (1992), *Reason and Culture. The Historic Role of Rationality and Rationalism*, Basil Blackwell, Oxford.

Glass, B. (1970), 'Maupertuis', *Dictionary of Scientific Biography*, Scribner, New York.

Gray, Alexander and A.E. Thompson (1980), *The Development of Economic Doctrine*, 2nd ed., Longman, London.

Groenewegen, P.D. (1977), *The Economics of A.R.J. Turgot*, Martinus Nijhoff, The Hague.

Groenewegen, P.D. (1983), 'Turgot's Place in the History of Economic Thought: A Bicentenary Estimate', *History of Political Economy*, vol. 15.

Halévy, Elie (1928), *The Growth of Philosophic Radicalism*, trans. by Mary Morris, Faber and Faber, London.

Hall, A. John (1986), *Powers and Liberties. The Causes and Consequences of the Rise of the West*, Basil Blackwell, Oxford.

Hall, R.L. and C.J. Hitch (1939), 'Price Theory and Business Behaviour', *Oxford Economic Papers*, vol. 1.

Hargreaves-Heap, Shaun (1989), *Rationality in Economics*, Basil Blackwell, Oxford.

Harrison, James (1971), 'Erasmus Darwin's Views of Evolution', *Journal of the History of Ideas*, vol. 32.

Harrod, F. (1966), *The Life of John Maynard Keynes*, Macmillan, London.

Harvey-Phillips, M.B. (1983), 'T.R. Malthus on the "Metaphysics of Political Economy": Ricardo's Critical Ally', in *Methodological Discussions in Economics: Historical Essays in Honor of T.W. Hutchison*, ed. by A.W. Coats, JAI Press, Greenwich, Connecticut.

Hecht, J. (1958), 'La Vie de François Quesnay', in *François Quesnay et la Physiocratie*, Institut National des Études Demographiques, Paris.

Helvétius, M. (1969), *A Treatise on Man; His Intellectual Faculties and His Education*, trans. by W. Hooper, Burt Franklin, New York.

Hicks, J. (1969), *A Theory of Economic History*, Clarendon Press, Oxford.

Hobbes, Thomas (1962), *Leviathan*, Collins, London.

Hollander, S. (1977), 'Adam Smith and the Self-Interest Axiom', *Journal of Law and Economics*, vol. 20.

Howitt, P. (1986), 'Conversations With Economists. A Review Essay', *Journal of Monetary Economics*, vol. 18.

Hume, David (1911), *A Treatise of Human Nature*, J.M. Dent and Sons, London.

Hume, David (1948), *Dialogues Concerning Natural Religion*, ed. by Henry D. Aiken, Hafner, New York.

Hume, David (1964), *The Philosophical Works*, ed. by T.H. Green and T.H. Grose, Scienta Verlag Allen, London.

Hume, David (1969), *The Letters of David Hume*, ed. by J.Y.T. Greig, Clarendon Press, Oxford.

Hume, David (1975), *Enquiries Concerning Human Understanding and Concerning the Principles of Morals*, ed. by L.A. Selby-Bigge and P.H. Nidditch, Clarendon Press, Oxford.

Hume, David (1987), *Essays, Moral, Political and Literary*, ed. by Eugene F. Miller, Liberty Classics, Indianapolis.

Huntley, William B. (1972), 'David Hume and Charles Darwin', *Journal of the History of Ideas*, vol. 33.

Hutcheson, Francis (1969), *A System of Moral Philosophy*, George Olms, Hildesheim.

Hutcheson, Francis (1971), *An Inquiry into the Original of Our Ideas of Beauty and Virtue*, Garland, New York.

Hutcheson, Francis (1973), *An Inquiry Concerning Beauty, Order, Harmony and Design*, ed. by Peter Krug, Martinus Nijhoff, The Hague.

Hutchison, Ross (1991), 'Locke in France - 1688-1734', *Studies on Voltaire and the Eighteenth Century*, vol. 290.

Hutchison, T.W. (1938), *The Significance and Basic Postulates of Economic Theory*, Macmillan, London.

James, E.D. (1975), 'Faith, Sincerity and Morality: Mandeville and Bayle' in Irwin Primer (ed.), *Mandeville Studies. New Explorations in the Art and Thought of Bernard Mandeville*, Martinus Nijhoff, The Hague.

Jones, Phillip S. (1970), 'Gabriel Cramer', in *Dictionary of Scientific Biography*, Scribner, New York.

Jones, Richard (1859), *Literary Remains: Consisting of Lectures and Tracts on Political Economy*, Murray, London.

Kaiser, Thomas E. (1989), 'The Abbé Dubos and the Historical Defence of the Monarchy in Early Eighteenth-Century France', *Studies on Voltaire and the Eighteenth Century*, vol. 267.

Kaplan, Steven L. (1976), *Bread, Politics and Political Economy in the Reign of Louis XV*, Martinus Nijhoff, The Hague.

Keynes, J.M. (1939), 'Professor Tinbergen's Methods', *Economic Journal*, vol. 49.

King, Lester S. (1970), *The Road to Medical Enlightenment 1650-1695*, MacDonald, London.

King, Lester S. (1976), 'Theory and Practice in 18th Century Medicine', *Studies on Voltaire and the Eighteenth Century*, vol. 133.

King, Lester S. (1978), *The Philosophy of Medicine*, Harvard University Press, Cambridge, Massachussetts.

Klamer, Arjo (1984), *The New Classical Macroeconomics: Conversations with the New Classical Economists and Their Opponents*, Wheatsheaf, Brighton.

Klein, Daniel (1985), 'Deductive Economic Methodology in the French Enlightenment: Condillac and Destutt de Tracy', *History of Political Economy*, vol. 17.

Korsmeyer, C. (1977), 'Is Pangloss Leibniz?', *Philosophy and Literature*, vol. 1.

Kubota, Akiteru (1958), 'Quesnay. Disciple de Malebranche', in *François Quesnay et la Physiocratie*, Institut National des Études Demographiques, Paris.

Landreth, Harry (1975), 'The Economic Thought of Bernard Mandeville', *History of Political Economy*, vol. 7.

Leibniz, G.W. (1951), *Theodicy*, ed. by Austin Farrer, trans. by E.M. Huggard, Routledge and Kegan Paul, London.

Leibniz, G.W. (1956), *The Leibniz-Clarke Correspondence*, ed. by H.G. Alexander, Manchester University Press, Manchester.

Leibniz, G.W. (1969), *Philosophical Papers and Letters* (2nd ed.), ed. by Leroy E. Loemker, D. Reidel, Dordrecht.

Leibniz, G.W. (1981), *New Essays on Human Understanding*, trans. by Peter Remnant and Johnathan Bennet, Cambridge University Press, Cambridge.

Leslie, T.E. Cliffe (1870), 'The Political Economy of Adam Smith', *The Fortnightly Review*, vol. 8.

Locke, John (1823), *The Works. A New Edition*, Thomas Tess, London.

Locke, John (1954), *Essays on the Law of Nature*, ed. by W. Von Leyden, Clarendon Press, Oxford.

Locke, John (1959), *An Essay Concerning Human Understanding*, ed. by Alexander Campbell Fraser, Dover, New York.

Locke, John (1976), *The Correspondence of John Locke*, ed. by E.S. DeBeer, Clarendon Press, Oxford.

Lombard, A. (1969), *L'Abbé Du Bos, Un Initiateur De La Pensée Moderne*, Slatkine Reprints, Geneva.

Lovejoy, A.O. (1909), 'The Argument for Organic Evolution Before the Origin of the Species, Parts 1 and 2', *Popular Science Monthly*, vol. 77.

Lovejoy, A.O. (1948), *Essays in the History of Ideas*, Johns Hopkins University Press, Baltimore.

Lovejoy, A.O. (1964), *The Great Chain of Being. A Study of the History of an Idea*, Harvard University Press, Cambridge, Massachusetts.

Lutfalla, Michael (1981), *Aux Origines de la Pensée Economique*, Economica, Paris.

Mach, Ernst (1960), *The Science of Mechanics: A Critical and Historical Account of its Development*, trans. by J. McCormack, Open Court, La Salle, Illinois.

Maistrov, L.E. (1974), *Probability Theory. A Historical Sketch*, ed. and trans. by Samuel Kotz, Academic Press, New York.

Malebranche, Nicolas (1980), *The Search After Truth*, trans. by Thomas M. Lennona and Paul J. Olscame, Ohio State University Press, Columbus.

Mandeville, Bernard (1924), *The Fable of the Bees: Or Private Vices, Publick Benefits*, ed. by F.B. Kaye, Clarendon Press, Oxford.

Mandeville, Bernard (1976), *A Treatise on the Hypochondriack and Hysterick Diseases*, Scholars' Facsimiles and Reprints, New York.

Marchi, N. De (1983), 'The Case for James Mill', *Methodological Discussions in Economics: Historical Essays in Honor of T.W. Hutchison*, ed. by A.W. Coats, JAI Press, Greenwich, Connecticut.

Maupertuis, Pierre-Louis Moreau de (1965), *Oeuvres*, Georg Olms, Hildesheim.

Maupertuis, Pierre-Louis Moreau de (1966), *The Earthly Venus*, trans. by S.B. Boas and introduced by G. Boas, Johnson Reprint Corporation, New York.

May, Louis Phillipe (1950), 'Descartes et les Physiocrates', *Revue de Synthèse*, vol. 27.

McCloskey, Donald N. (1983), 'The Rhetoric of Economics', *Journal of Economic Literature*, vol. 21.

Meek, Ronald L. (1971), 'Smith, Turgot and the "Four Stages" Theory', *History of Political Economy*, vol. 3.

Meghill, A.D. (1975), 'Theory and Experience in Adam Smith', *Journal of the History of Ideas*, vol. 36.

Mercier de la Rivière, P.-P. (1910), *L'Ordre Naturel et Essential des Sociétés Politiques*, Paul Geuthner, Paris.

Mill, James (1869), *Analysis of the Phenomena of the Human Mind*, Longmans Green Reade and Dyer, London.

Mill, John Stuart (1844), *Essays on Some Unsettled Questions of Political Economy*, John W. Parker, London.

Mill, John Stuart (1980), *Mill on Bentham and Coleridge*, Cambridge University Press, Cambridge.

Mini, Piero V. (1974), *Philosophy and Economics: The Origins and Development of Economic Theory*, University Presses of Florida, Gainesville.

Mizuta, Hiroshi (1967), *Adam Smith's Library*, Cambridge University Press, Cambridge.

Montesquieu, Charles-Louis de Secondat (1949), *Oeuvres Complètes*, ed. by Roger Caillois, Gallimard, Paris.

Montesquieu, Charles-Louis de Secondat (1989), *The Spirit of the Laws*, trans. by Anne M. Cohler, Basia Carolyn Miller and Harold Samuel Stone, Cambridge University Press, Cambridge.

Morrow, Glenn R. (1969), *The Ethical and Economic Theories of Adam Smith*, Augustus M. Kelley, New York.

Myers, M.L. (1972), 'Philosophical Anticipations of Laissez-Faire', *History of Political Economy*, vol. 4.

Neill, Thomas P. (1948), 'Quesnay and Physiocracy', *Journal of the History of Ideas*, vol. 9.

Neill, Thomas P. (1949), 'The Physiocrats' Concept of Economics', *Quarterly Journal of Economics*, vol. 63.

Oake, R.B. (1940), 'Did Maupertuis Read Hume's Treatise on Human Nature?', *Revue de Littérature Comparée*, vol. 20.

Oncken, A. (1897), 'The Consistency of Adam Smith', *Economic Journal*, vol. 7.

Pareto, Vilfredo (1935), *The Mind and Society*, trans. by A. Bongiorno, A. Livingstone and J.H. Rogers, Cape, London.

Petty, William (1808), 'The Advice of William Petty to Mr Samuel Hartlib for the Advancement of Some Particular Parts of Learning', *The Harleian Miscellany*, John White, London.

Petty, William (1899), *The Economic Writing of Sir William Petty*, ed. by Charles Henry Hull, Cambridge University Press, Cambridge.

Petty, William (1927), *The Petty Papers*, ed. by Maquis de Landsdowne, Constable, London.

Pokorny, D. (1978), 'Smith and Walras: Two Theories of Science', *Canadian Journal of Economics*, vol. 11.

Popkin, Richard R. (1967), 'Bernard Mandeville', ed. by Paul Edwards, *Encyclopedia of Philosophy*, vol. 5.

Primer, Irwin (1975), 'Mandeville and Shaftesbury: Some Facts and Problems' in Irwin Primer (ed.), *Mandeville Studies. New*

Explorations in the Art and Thought of Bernard Mandeville, Martinus Nijhoff, The Hague.

Quesnay, François (1736), *Essai Physique sur l'Économie Animale*, Paris.

Quesnay, François (1888), *Oeuvres Économiques et Philosophiques*, ed. by Auguste Oncken, Joseph Baer, Frankfurt.

Quesnay, François (1946), *Despotism in China*, trans. by Lewis A. Maverick, Paul Anderson, San Antonio.

Quesnay, François (1958), 'Evidence', in *François Quesnay et la Physiocratie*, Institut Nationale des Études Demographiques, Paris.

Rae, John (1965), *Life of Adam Smith*, Augustus M. Kelley, New York.

Rashid, Salim (1985), 'Dugald Stewart, "Baconian" Methodology and Political Economy', *Journal of the History of Ideas*, vol. 45.

Reid, Thomas (1785), *Essays on the Intellectual Powers of Man*, Scolar Press, Menston.

Ricardo, David (1952), *The Works and Correspondence of David Ricardo*, ed. by Piero Sraffa, Cambridge University Press, Cambridge.

Robbins, Lionel (1935), *An Essay on the Nature and Significance of Economic Science*, Macmillan, London.

Romanell, Patrick (1984), *John Locke and Medicine: A New Key to Locke*, 2nd ed., Prometheus Books, New York.

Rousseau G.S. (1972), 'Sowing the Wind, and Reaping the Whirlwind: Aspects of Change in Eighteenth-Century Medicine. Aspects of English Intellectual History 1640-1800', in Paul J. Korshin (ed.), *Studies in Change and Revolution: Aspects of English Intellectual History, 1640-1800*, Scolar Press, Mensten.

Rousseau, G.S. (1975), 'Mandeville and Europe: Medicine and Philosophy', in Irwin Primer (ed.), *Mandeville Studies. New Explorations in the Art and Thought of Dr Bernard Mandeville*, Martinus Nijhoff, The Hague.

Samuelson, Paul A. (1959), 'What Economists Know', in D. Lerner (ed.), *The Human Meaning of the Social Sciences*, Meridian Books, New York.

Samuelson, Paul A. (1972), 'Maximum Principles in Economics', *The Collected Scientific Papers of Paul Samuelson*, volume 3, MIT Press, Cambridge.

Samuelson Paul A. (1977), 'St. Petersburg Paradoxes: Defanged, Dissected and Historically Described', *Journal of Economic Literature*, vol. 15.

Say, J. (1865), *Treatise on Political Economy: or, The Production, Distribution and Consumption of Wealth*, Lippincott, Philadelphia.

Schneck, Jerome M. (1957), 'Thomas Sydenham and Psychological Medicine', *American Journal of Psychiatry*, vol. 113.

Schumpeter, Joseph A. (1954a), *History of Economic Analysis*, Oxford University Press, New York.

Schumpeter, Joseph A. (1954b), *Economic Doctrine and Method. A Historical Sketch*, trans. by R. Aris, George Allen and Unwin, London.

Scott, William Robert (1937), *Adam Smith as Student and Professor*, Jackson and Son, Glasgow.

Scott, William Robert (1966), *Francis Hutcheson. His Life, Teaching and Position in the History of Philosophy*, Augustus M. Kelley, New York.

Sen, S.R. (1957), *The Economics of Sir James Steuart*, G. Bell and Sons, London.

Shackleton, Robert (1955), 'The Evolution of Montesquieu's Theory of Climate', *Revue Internationale de Philosophie*.

Shackleton, Robert (1961), *Montesquieu, A Critical Biography*, Oxford University Press, Oxford.

Shaftesbury, Anthony Cooper, Earl of (1900), *The Life, Unpublished Letters and Philosophical Regimen of Anthony, Earl of Shaftesbury*, ed. by Benjamin R and, Swan Sonnenschien, London.

Skidelsky, R. (1992), *John Maynard Keynes: A Biography*, vol. 2, Macmillan, London.

Skinner, O. (1969), 'Meaning and Understanding in the History of Ideas', *History and Theory*, vol. 8.

Smith, Adam (1937), *An Inquiry Into The Nature and Causes of the Wealth of Nations*, ed. by Edwin Cannan, The Modern Library, New York.

Smith, Adam (1978), *Lectures on Jurisprudence*, ed. by R.L. Meek, R.D. Raphael and P.S. Stein, Clarendon Press, Oxford.

Smith, Adam (1982a), *Essays on Philosophical Subjects*, ed. by W.P.D. Wightman and J.C. Bryce, Liberty Classics, Indianapolis.

Smith, Adam (1982b), *The Theory of Moral Sentiments*, ed. by D.D. Raphael and A.L. Macfie, Liberty Classics, Indianapolis.

Smith, Adam (1985), *Lectures on Rhetoric and Belles Lettres*, ed. by J.C. Bryce and A.S. Skinner, Liberty Classics, Indianapolis.

Smith, Adam (1987), *The Correspondence of Adam Smith*, ed. by Ernest Campbell Mossner and Ian Simpson Ross, Liberty Classics, Indianapolis.

Spiegel, Henry W. (1975), 'A Note on the Equilibrium Concept in the History of Economics', *Economie Appliquée*, vol. 28.

Spiegel Henry W. (1979), 'Adam Smith's Heavenly City', in Gerald P. O'Driscoll (ed.), *Adam Smith and Modern Political Economy. Bicentennial Essays on the Wealth of Nations*, Iowa State University Press, Ams.

Stark, W. (1943), *The Ideal Foundations of Economic Thought*, Routledge and Kegan Paul, London.

Stark, W. (1944), *The History of Economics in its Relation to Social Development*, Kegan Paul, Trench and Trubner, London.

Stark, W. (1960), *Montesquieu: Pioneer of the Sociology of Knowledge,* Routledge and Kegan Paul, London.

Steuart, James (1966), *An Inquiry into the Principles of Political Economy*, ed. by Andrew S. Skinner, Oliver and Boyd, Edinburgh.

Stewart, Dugald (1867), *The Elements of the Philosophy of the Human Mind*, Tess, London.

Streissler, Erich W. (1990), 'The Influence of German Economics on the Work of Menger and Marshall', in B.J. Caldwell (ed.) *Carl Menger and His Legacy*, Duke University Press, Durham.

Strenski, E.M. (1967), 'Diderot, for and against the Physiocrats', *Studies on Voltaire and the Eighteenth Century*, vol. 57.

Sutter, Jean (1958), 'Quesnay et la Médecine', *François Quesnay et la Physiocratie*, Institut Nationale Des Études Demographiques, Paris.

Taine, Hippolyte Adolphe (1876), *The Ancient Regime*, trans. by John Durand, Henry Holt, USA.

Taylor, W.L. (1965), *Francis Hutcheson and David Hume as Predecessors of Adam Smith*, Duke University Press, Durham, North Carolina.

Temkin, Owsei (1991), *Hippocrates in a World of Pagans and Christians*, Johns Hopkins University Press, Baltimore.

Thaler, Richard H. (1992), *The Winner's Curse: Paradoxes and Anomalies of Economic Life*, Free Press, New York.

Turgot, A.R.J. (1913), *Oeuvres de Turgot et Documents le Concernant*, ed. by Gustave Schelle, F. Alcan, Paris.

Turgot, A.R.J. (1973), *Turgot on Progress, Sociology and Economics*, ed. by Ronald L. Meek, Cambridge University Press, Cambridge.

Turgot, A.R.J. (1992), *Turgot. Extracts From His Economic Correspondence 1765-1768*, ed. by P.D. Groenewegen, Reprints of Economic Classics, series 2, number 6, University of Sydney, Sydney.

Vaihinger, H. (1924), *The Philosophy of 'As If'*, trans. by C.K. Ogden, Kegan Paul, Trench and Trubner, London.

Veblen, Thorstein (1964), *What Veblen Taught. Selected Writings Of Thorstein Veblen*, ed. by Wesley C. Mitchell, Augustus M. Kelley, New York.

Venturi, Franco (1972), *Italy and the Enlightenment: Studies in a Cosmopolitan Century*, trans. by Susan Corsi, New York University Press, New York.

Verri, P. (1986), *Reflections on Political Economy*, trans. by B. McGilvray and P.D. Groenewegen, Reprints of Economic Classics, series 2, number 6, University of Sydney, Sydney.

Viner, Jacob (1953), 'Introduction', in: *A Letter to Dion*, by Bernard Mandeville, The Augustan Reprint Society, Los Angeles.

Viner, Jacob (1972), *The Role of Providence in the Social Order : An Essay in Intellectual History*, American Philosophical Society, Philadelphia.

Voltaire (1943), *Lettres Philosophiques*, ed. by F.A. Taylor, Basil Blackwell, Oxford.

Voltaire (1877), *Oeuvres Complètes de Voltaire*, ed. by Louis Moland, Garnier, Paris.

Waddell, D. (1958-1959), 'Charles Davenant (1656-1714) - A Biographical Sketch', *The Economic History Review*, vol. 11.

Whewell, William (1967), *History of the Inductive Sciences*, Frank Cass, London.

Index